Peanut Butter & Jelly

Gloria —
All the best as you live out Vancouver and beyond. God bless. Keep up the perfect daughter facade!

Mike
8/17

All Bible quotations in this publication are taken from The Message (MSG).

Just As I Am by Billy Graham, copyright © 2007. Used by permission of HarperOne. All rights reserved.

The Message by Eugene H. Peterson, copyright © 1993, 1994, 1995, 1996, 2000, 2001, 2002. Used by permission of NavPress Publishing Group. All rights reserved.

Passion and Purity by Elisabeth Elliot, copyright © 1984. Used by permission of Fleming H. Revell, a division of Baker Book House Company. All rights reserved.

I Love You, Ronnie: The Letters of Ronald Reagan to Nancy Reagan by Nancy Reagan, copyright © 2002. Used by permission of Random House. All rights reserved.

All stories described are true though some names, relationships, and locations have been changed to protect identity.

No animals were harmed or tested on in the production of this book.

Disclaimer: Read this book at your own risk. The writer and illustrator are not responsible if you apply this book and mess up your life.

Peanut Butter & Jelly

How to Find a Match Made in Heaven

Mike Toy & Audrey Jung

iUniverse, Inc.
New York Bloomington

Peanut Butter & Jelly
How to Find a Match Made in Heaven

Copyright © 2008 by Mike Toy

All rights reserved. No part of this book may be used or reproduced by any means, graphic, electronic, or mechanical, including photocopying, recording, taping or by any information storage retrieval system without the written permission of the publisher except in the case of brief quotations embodied in critical articles and reviews.

iUniverse books may be ordered through booksellers or by contacting:

iUniverse
1663 Liberty Drive
Bloomington, IN 47403
www.iuniverse.com
1-800-Authors (1-800-288-4677)

Because of the dynamic nature of the Internet, any Web addresses or links contained in this book may have changed since publication and may no longer be valid. The views expressed in this work are solely those of the author and do not necessarily reflect the views of the publisher, and the publisher hereby disclaims any responsibility for them.

ISBN: 978-0-595-39287-2 (pbk)
ISBN: 978-0-595-83680-2 (ebk)

Printed in the United States of America

Contents

Dedication vii

Thank You ix

Hear Ye! Hear Ye! xi

Welcome xiii

Book 1 How to Ask a Girl Out—For Guys Only 1

Part 1: Are You Ready? 3
    1) Following God 3
    2) Preparing Your Heart 5
    3) Why Guys Don't Ask 7
    4) What Do I Look For? 8
    5) Victory in the Asking 10

Part 2: Go for It 13
    6) How to Be a Scintillating Conversationalist 13
    7) How to Develop a Sense of Humor 16
    8) Just Do It 20
    9) How to Ask a Girl Out 24
    10) Getting to Know Her 32

Part 3: Understanding Girl-Talk 35
    11) What She Really Means 35
    12) Walking on Eggs 36

Part 4: When She Gives You a Lemon 40
    13) When She Says No 40
    14) Pursuing the Girl 42
    15) Un-Breaking Your Heart 43
    16) Life Goes On 45

Part 5: When She Says Yes 47
    17) DTR: Define the Relationship 47

Book 2 How to Kiss the Right Frog—For Girls Only 51
    1) Loving God 53
    2) Don't Read Into Things 54
    3) How to Win a Guy's Attention 55

    4) How to Make Yourself Approachable 57
    5) Right Place at the Right Time 60
    6) Clearly Communicating 62
    7) Let's Just Be Friends. 64
    8) Staying True. 66
    9) Don't Tell the Whole World. 67
    10) Only Once 68

Book 3 How to Find True Love .69
    1) A Day to Remember 71
    2) What is Marriage? 73
    3) Gotta-Have Qualities. 74
    4) Nice-to-Have Qualities 75
    5) 10 Things You Don't Wanna Do 76
    6) Giving Love a Chance 81

Book 4 Got Love?—Questions & Answers 83
    1) Dating. 85
    2) Expectations 91
    3) Conflicts 93
    4) Differences. 94
    5) Parents' Blessings 95
    6) Counseling 96

Book 5 Bonus Section: Extra! Extra! Read All About It! 99

Part 1—Just For Kicks. 101
    1) Social Etiquette for the Clueless. 101
    2) How to Tell if a Guy Likes You 125
    3) Why Men Are Just Happier People 128
    4) The Secrets of Women's Language 130
    5) Top 10 Worse Ways to Start A DTR 132
    6) Bubba's List 133
    7) Boys to Men Boot Camp. 138
    8) When I Fall in Love. 141

Part 2—Insights 145
    1) Before You Say "I Do". 145
    2) My Journey in Understanding Girls. 160
    3) Recommended Resources. 166

About the Illustrator 169

About the Writer. 169

Dedication

Joseph Ng & David Lee

From a heart which can never fully express just how deeply grateful I am…

Thank you for helping me be all I can for Jesus.

Thank You

Gosh! I want to thank all my friends who have made this book possible.

Girls:

Vivian Gee, Allison Fong, Lil Wong, Emily Wu, Ellen Wu, Stephanie Ng, Kalam Lok, Jenny Lee, Traci Shirachi, Susan Lee, Jennifer Toy, Cindy Wang, Taryn Moy, Chai Lee, Melissa Wong, Stephanie Mung, Charlene Chan, Christine Wong, Thao Nguyen, Florence Tse, Vanessa Wong, Jennifer King, Alice Mui, Rebecca Yen, Annie Shen, Ann Ku, Sarah Howard, Susan Osborn, Cindy Zhou, Ya Mei Li, Joyce Wang, Indah Ratna, Karen Panyalertrat, Cindy Feng, Lucy Yang, Ellen Joe, Jennifer Lee, Giselle Dineros, Alicia Liu, Pearl Moy, Julia Fong, Marianne Lee, Angie Ng, May Lynn Chang, Karen Lin, Anny Chang, Grace Cheng, Judy Lee, Jenny Yoo, Sally Stuart, Tama Westman, Annie Cheng, Munglen Hsiao, Candice So, Sara Rodriguez, Diane Ngo, Suzanne Harlan, Carrie Graham, Heidi Oh, Peggy Tsai, Gloria Chiu, Stella Aung, Briana Shimada, Beth Gee, Jessica Oei, Joanne Ding, Kelie Kang, Sakura Suzuki, Hannah Whang, Paula Wu, Liz Chang, Karen Liu, Juliana Wang, Cathy Sin, Elisa Lui, Anna Chao, and Emily Wang.

Guys:

John Voelker, Chris Cheung, Takashi Matsukawa, David Lee, John Chuang, Dale Kim, Michael Yee, Joe Fassler, Matthew Kwok, Mike Hamada, John Cheng, Bryan Lee, Brian Toy, Peter Nguyen, Chris Perry, Andy Lau, Vince Chan, Wah Ping Luk, Jason Wong, Donny Pusawong, Mike Hong, Tom Hui, Tak Huang, Albert Cheng, Matt Kwok, Jeffrey Lam, Joseph Au, Jeff Vreeland, Eddy Liao, Edmund Young, Rio Chang, Joseph Ng, Jon Trebilco, Leonard Moy, Lee Warren, Zachary Howard, Joey Chao, John Yang, Dave Krommenhoek, Kevin Maynard, Jonathan Pon, Jef Jung, Tim Mak, Abe Lewis, Bob Goldmann, Donny Chan, Kai Shen, Nelson Chau, Wayne Hsu, and Kai Wing Leung.

Peanut Butter & Jelly

Couples:

Sen & June Wong, John & Sakura Lee, Mat & Janet Jung, Pira & Venus Tritasavit, Tom & Amanda Sugimura, Eric & Pam Yata, Gary & Tracy Lee, Alex & Susan Jung, Lee & Miltinnie Yih, Alan & Connie Cheng, Paul & Lis Lam, Phil & Mary Ann Shui, Alfred & Julie Leong, Darren & Suzy Tom, Jackson & Cynthia Wan, Alan & Beverly Ginn, Dalon & Eva Chin, Dana & Susan Chau, Gary & Flora Wong, Kelly & Shirley Ng, Peter & Polly Lee, Sherman & Karen Lim, Joel & Maria Arpilleda, Jerry & Margaret Wong, Tommy & Pam Tse, Simon & Joyce Lee, Lucas & Serena Ng, Albert & Christie Chong, Danny & Patti Mar, Kenny & Cindy Chau, Peter & Jamie Ong, David & Lia Huynh, Vieng & Sally Wong, Andrew & Sophia Suwidgi, Byron & Maria Wang, Dick & Donna Andrews, Matt & Angel Dillane, Ralph & Mary Leong, John & Sakura Lee, Mason & Debbie Shih, Dave & Peggy Pardini, Peter & Kristine Yim, KJ & Brenda Jung, Rob & Debbie Schwartz, Victor & Elinna Choy, Ralph & Marilyn Bagshaw, Tim & Becky Lewis, Mike & Vanji Taron, Tom & Dana Steers, Dylan & Beth Clendenin, Jason & Sarah Kerner, Lawrence & Sharon Huey, Daniel & Christine Wong, Aaron & Rachael Vorbau, Chris & Rebecca Tihon, Andrew & Bernice Chee, Walt & Leette Henrichsen, and WALL·E & EVE.

Theresa Armada, my high school English teacher, thanks for showing me how to say the same thing better.

Audrey Jung, you are an amazing artist.

Mama & Papa, your marriage is inspirational.

Jesus, I have no life apart from you.

Hear Ye! Hear Ye!

"Alas, a dating book that delivers both spiritual principles on relationships and practical words of wisdom. Mike's priceless tips on how to ask for a date and boy-girl communication are insightful and applicable. His witty, laugh-out-loud humor makes this an easy and enjoyable read for single guys and girls of all ages."

Brian Toy, Little Brother

"All I have to say is that this book is the bomb."

Jennifer Toy, Little Sister

(Note: Neither Brian, nor Jennifer were paid, nor coerced into writing this endorsement.)

Welcome

Dear Friend,

Thanks for picking this book up. You're in store for a real adventure.

Peanut Butter & Jelly. Has there ever been a better match made in heaven? I bet you want that match, too, huh?

Well, after seven years of extensive research and writing, you have advice at your fingertips that will aid you for life. This book is five books in one. Well, technically it's four books, plus I'm going to throw in the bonus section just because you're you. Awww. Don't you feel special? You should… because you are.

Here is what you're getting:

1) How to Ask a Girl Out—For Guys Only
2) How to Kiss the Right Frog—For Girls Only
3) How to Find True Love
4) Got Love?—Questions & Answers
5) Bonus Section: Extra! Extra! Read All About It!

I hope you find this light-hearted read fun and entertaining. My prayer is that they will draw you closer to God and that God will draw you one step closer to the one He created for you.

Delightfully Yours,

Mike Toy

San Francisco, California

Book 1
How to Ask a Girl Out—For Guys Only

Part 1: Are You Ready?

1) Following God

Do You Follow Hard After God?

Kind of a hard question to answer, huh? Notice the question wasn't any of the following:

- "Do you pray?"
- "Do you read the Bible?"
- "Do you regularly go to church?"
- "Do you help out with church functions?"

In and of themselves, these activities do not necessarily indicate anything about your spiritual health. Surprised?

You might be wondering, "What does this have anything to do with asking a girl out?" Lots. Let me tell you why. If God really is who the Bible claims He is—the Creator of all life, Giver of joy, magnificent, and beautiful, then to have everything in this world minus God would be to have nothing at all.

"All the things I once thought were so important are gone from my life. Compared to the high privilege of knowing Christ Jesus as my Master, firsthand, everything I once thought I had going for me is insignificant—dog dung. I've dumped it all in the trash so that I could embrace Christ."[1]

Dog dung. Life without God is dog dung. If you do not treasure God above everything else in life, then you are missing out on the greatest treasure of

---

1   Philippians 3:8-9

all. You can even have the bestest[2] girlfriend in the world and be missing out. Sound strange? Well, not if you really think about it.

Life is about God.[3] Short, simple, and sweet. It's not first and foremost about how to get a girl to hold your hand or convince her you are God's gift to women. If your life is not characterized by heartfelt obedience and desire to glorify God, then perhaps you need to take a break from the dating scene and first ask God to give you a spiritual heart. Sound a little extreme?

If God is the One who truly satisfies and you're not satisfied in Him, what makes you think you'll be any more satisfied with a girlfriend? Get your priorities straight. Beg and plead with God to renew a passion in your heart for Him. If your heart doesn't beat for the things on God's heart, you have no business asking a girl out. First thing first, guys.

We all know God ought to be first in our lives, but talk is cheap. Anyone can talk the talk. You've got to ask yourself, "Is the earnest desire of my heart to follow hard after Jesus?"

If God is important to you, then whatever is on God's heart would be important to you, too, namely, people. Ask yourself, "Do I go out of my way to serve and help others?"

If you want this to describe you, ask God to help.

Here's a simple prayer you can say from your heart:

Lord,

I constantly wander away from you, but I want to follow you. Won't you help me? Lead me and I will follow. Give me the strength and energy, O God. Help me keep my eyes on you.

Amen.

---

2   This word means the best of the best. I made this word up myself. Pretty creative, huh?

3   If you don't know God, you can have a relationship with Him right now. Just say with your heart, "I believe you, O God." It's that simple. If that's your heart's prayer, congratulations! Now, just follow God's desire for your life (found in the Bible) all your days. Told you it was simple!

2) Preparing Your Heart

Let me ask you a question.

Why do you want to ask a girl out in the first place?

Common responses may include:

- "I'm lonely."
- "She's fun to be with."
- "I want someone to talk to."
- "She makes me feel special."
- "Well, everybody else is coupling up."

If these are your best answers, you have a serious problem. Why? Because these are inadequate.

The reason why you do anything is to glorify God. You might say, "Well, that was assumed." Before you make your case, think about this a little further. If it really were assumed, then wouldn't you have at least thought about it? Usually, you don't because you don't really believe it is.

"... Do everything... heartily and freely to God's glory."[4]

Everything we do is to glorify God. But how might this look like? Well, since she is your sister-in-Christ, do the one-anothers (i.e. love one another, serve one another, encourage one another...) and point her to God. If this is not a big part of why you're asking her out, step back and evaluate why not?

Wanting to get to know a girl only because she is cute can be self-serving. I'm not saying attraction and chemistry are not important. They most certainly are, but even more importantly, we are to have a Christ-like attitude.

"So if I, the Master and Teacher, washed your feet, you must now wash each other's feet."[5]

Serve her by getting to know her and her needs. If you're not planning to do this, please don't ask her out. Some guys think hanging out with a girl

---

4   1 Corinthians 10:31
5   John 13:14

Peanut Butter & Jelly

is OK, but if your goal is not to bless and encourage her, you're wasting her time. Set your relationship with God as top priority and everything else will fall into its proper place.

Asking a girl out can be nerve-wracking. A million things may race through your mind including:

- "What if she likes me?"
- "What if she doesn't like me?"
- "What if she is shocked when I ask her out?"
- "What if our friendship becomes a bit awkward if things don't pan out?"
- "What if she tells all her friends I asked her out? Wouldn't that embarrass me?"
- "What if she is only interested in being 'just friends'?"

The what-if list can go on and on. It's only normal for you to worry and be anxious. This is a great time to turn to the Lord for help and guidance.

"Don't fret or worry. Instead of worrying, pray. Let petitions and praises shape your worries into prayers, letting God know your concerns. Before you know it, a sense of God's wholeness, everything coming together for good, will come and settle you down. It's wonderful what happens when Christ displaces worry at the center of your life."[6]

Did you know God cares for you? Stop to think about that for a minute. What a thought, huh? The God who upholds all the stars in the sky, all the galaxies in the world, all the planets in orbit, would care about a little shrimp like you? Wow! I don't know about you, but that floors me. Why wouldn't I want to cast my anxieties on such a God?

Even though God knows all your needs before you ask, you still ought to present your requests to Him. Telling God about your needs or worries is for your own good. Laying everything down at His feet is a way of worshiping Him. The focus becomes less on you and your worries, and more on Him and His ways.

The promise of God's wholeness and peace is yours when you tell God your requests. This feeling is not something the world understands. It transcends understanding. It is the sense of well-being that even though circumstances may be harsh and crazy, God is good, in control, and cares for you.

6   Philippians 4:6-7

3) Why Guys Don't Ask

Guys don't ask girls out for myriads of reasons. Let's just highlight a few common ones:

- Fear of rejection

    No one wants to be turned down for a date.

- Fear of awkwardness

    If a girl says no, things can get a little weird. If other people know the guy asked the girl out, that makes it even more uncomfortable.

- Fear of commitment

    Some guys don't want to give up the freedom of being unattached. They might not be ready to look after someone else.

- Unhealthy career preoccupation

    Going to graduate school or working up the corporate ladder is fine, but that's all some guys can think about.

- Lack of perceived interest on the girl's part

    The less interest a girl shows in a guy, the less interested a guy would be in the girl. He might think, "Why should I ask a girl out who is obviously not interested in me?"

- Lack of maturity

    Guys just don't grow up as fast as girls. Some are lifetime Toys 'R Us kids.

- Lack of godly girls

    "A good woman is hard to find, and worth far more than diamonds."[7]

While some are legitimate reasons, others are not. If you struggle with asking a girl out, ask yourself what your hang up is so you can work on it.

---

[7] Proverbs 31:10

Peanut Butter & Jelly

Here are some questions to reflect on:

- "What is holding me back from asking a girl out?"
- "Should it hold me back?"
- "What do my friends think my problem is?"
- "What do my friends think the solution is?"
- "What can I do to overcome confidence hurdles?"
- "What does my past dating experience tell me about myself?"

4) What Do I Look For?

At the bare minimum, the girl you're looking for should be a professing believer. This doesn't mean you should go for any Christian girl out there. Just because a girl is "Christian" doesn't necessarily tell you anything about the quality of her relationship with God. The Bible never says it is wrong to date[8] an unbeliever, but it does say believers are not to marry unbelievers.

---

8   The concept of dating does not appear in the Bible. Dating emerged in the United States at the turn of the 20th century… at least this is what my friend told me.

"Don't become partners with those who reject God. How can you make a partnership out of right and wrong? That's not partnership; that's war. Is light best friends with dark? Does Christ go strolling with the Devil? Do trust and mistrust hold hands?"[9]

This isn't suggesting that you shouldn't have friends who don't share your faith. On the contrary, a believer's influence on this world is dependent upon the quality of relationships he has with the ones who don't share his faith.

This is saying that you are not to be in partnerships that cannot be broken with those who don't share your faith in God. This would include marriage and any emotional relationships where you want something so bad you cannot let go. For this reason, guard your heart and feelings from girls who don't share your faith.

You only have so much heart in you. The more heart you give to various girls, the less heart you'll have left for your wife one day. You, especially, don't want to give your heart to a girl who wants nothing to do with God.

If you are not careful, what happened to Solomon, former King of Israel, may happen to you.

"King Solomon was obsessed with women. Pharaoh's daughter was only the first of the many foreign women he loved... He took them from the surrounding pagan nations of which GOD had clearly warned Israel, 'You must not marry them; they'll seduce you into infatuations with their gods.' Solomon fell in love with them anyway, refusing to give them up... And they did seduce him away from God. As Solomon grew older, his wives beguiled him with their alien gods and he became unfaithful—he didn't stay true to his GOD as his father David had done... Solomon openly defied GOD; he did not follow in his father David's footsteps."[10]

Poor Solomon. He could have been a great king for his country, but because he didn't guard his heart from his sinful inclinations he started drifting farther and farther away from God and pursuing godless women. Likewise, dating an unbeliever may sway your heart away from God.

The kind of girls you are interested in tells you about your standards. If you are willing to date an unbeliever or a "Christian" who is apathetic about God, this tells you about your spiritual health. If you are striving to be like

---

9 2 Corinthians 6:14-15
10 1 Kings 11:1-6

Jesus in all your ways only girls who are also doing the same will attract you. Guard your heart from falling for the wrong girls.

5) Victory in the Asking

By asking a girl out, did you know you have already won? You're victorious. You're probably thinking, "But what if she says no?" Even if she says no, you're still a champ. Victory does not depend on the outcome. Rather, victory is in the asking. It comes when you ask a girl out, "Wanna get some chow mein?"[11]

Free tip: When you ask a girl out, sound excited even if you're nervous.

A date doesn't necessarily have to be a candlelight dinner at some fancy hilltop restaurant. Nope. It can be a casual hang out to get to know someone you're interested in. This could be having coffee, a picnic at the park, going to a museum; the possibilities are endless.

To set the record straight, just because you get a date with a girl doesn't officially make you boyfriend-girlfriend. Yeah, this should be obvious, but for some of you newbies it might not be. If this wasn't, let's pretend I just hit you over your head. ***Pop*** Hurts, huh? Well, you deserved it.

---

11 Peter Parker used this line on Mary Jane Watson in Spider-man. Classic!

Having the guts or courage to ask is a sign of a real warrior, a true champion, a winner. Don't be like the bucketsful of guys who are easily satisfied with superficial relationships with girls that go nowhere. That's just not cool. You can learn so much neat stuff from girls you won't get from guys.

Asking a girl out is a privilege. To be a man and not take initiative, not just with girls, but in other areas in life, truly robs a man of his spirit, the essence of being a man. You only have one life to live. That's it. One life.

If you want to get to know a girl better, do so. Don't keep putting it off. God has given you only so many days to live, so live it up. How sad it would be to look back one day and wonder, "Gosh, I wish I had gotten to know Beatrice better. If only I asked her out." Don't live in regret. Live as though there is no tomorrow. Live each moment to the hilt. Be Indiana Jones.

Part 2: Go for It

6) How to Be a Scintillating Conversationalist

Conversation is an art.

Become an interesting person. If you're not spontaneous and need to prepare, take time to think of how you can be fun and exciting before you go to a function (i.e. party, social, dinner…). Come up with some cool conversation topics. You don't enjoy looking at boring art, do you? Then why not become a master artist in conversation. Get it, Picasso?

World-renowned relationship expert Kate Chan shares the following insightful tips. Practice makes perfect.

You have just mustered up enough courage to approach "Someone of Great Interest" (SGI). Now what do you do?

Peanut Butter & Jelly

This is where the art of conversation comes in...

Conversation is a little like playing a game of ping-pong, (not the kind where you're trying to take out your opponent... well, unless the person is really into debating, or enjoys a battle of wits), but the kind where you are just volleying the ball back and forth to each other over the net.

Have you ever had the experience of being in a conversation with someone who merely offers one-word or one-sentence answers to all of your questions? This feels a little like volleying a ball over the net, and instead of passing the ball back, the other person just lets the ball fall to the ground.

Girl: "Where are you from?"

Guy: "San Francisco."

Girl: "What do you do?"

Guy: "Engineering."

Girl: "Do you like your job?"

Guy: "It's alright."

(Silence.)

Girl: "Well, I'm going to get a drink now..."

You keep on hitting balls to them over the net, but the balls just keep on falling to the ground. Pretty soon you run out of balls and you get bored and don't want to play anymore.

In the art of conversation, one should learn to respond with more than just a one-word answer. If possible, elaborate on your answer. It may lead the conversation into other more interesting, unexplored territory—thereby giving your conversation partner something from which to spring-board off of...

Girl: "Where are you from?"

Guy: "San Francisco, but I grew up in New York."

Girl: "Really? What brings you out here?"

Guy: "I really love the weather and the people here, so when I got transferred out here I couldn't say, 'No'."

Girl: "Yeah, I think we're spoiled with good weather here. So how do you like California compared to New York?"

Guy: Well, I actually just moved here so I haven't really had a chance to do all those tourist things like walk the Golden Gate Bridge or go to Fisherman's Wharf. Are there any places worth visiting?

Girl: Omigosh, yeah! In fact, my friends and I can show you around next weekend if you like. Sound good?

Guy: Oh great! I really look forward to it. Hope the weather will be nice like today.

On the other side of the net, one should also learn to ask good questions. Open-ended questions, which require more than just a one-word answer, are best.

Too often I hear the complaint that people end up having the same conversation over and over again at a party. ("Where are you from?", "What do you do?", "Which college did you go to?", etc., etc.) After that, people are at a loss for words.

So learn to ask interesting and thought-provoking questions that perhaps even get at a person's deeper values. (Hint: Can't think of good questions? The Book of Questions and 1001 Conversation Starters are great resources.)

Find ways to relate to the other person's experiences and share about your own experiences. By relating to and with another person, you are building rapport and forming connections with that person.

Be an attentive listener. Ask clarifying questions to let the person know you are tracking with them. This also encourages him or her to share further.

Be careful not to hog all the air-time. Sometimes people talk a lot or ramble when they are nervous. If you find that you are talking too much, stop and ask the other person a question and listen attentively.

7) How to Develop a Sense of Humor

When I survey girls and ask them what qualities they like in a guy there is one that comes up all the time. Can you guess what it is? Yup, you got it. A sense of humor.

Why is a sense of humor so important? Well, girls enjoy a good laugh. They're looking for guys who are fun and interesting. I want you to be that guy.

Ever since I was a kid, I loved making people laugh. When I was starting off, my sense of humor wasn't all that great. People didn't think I was that funny because I didn't deliver the punch line right. They asked, "Was that a joke?" Ouch.

Over the years, I've improved my batting average. If you want to hit the ball out of the park, don't give up. Just keep working on that swing and eventually you'll connect and everyone will like you. You can do it.

Let's talk about a few styles of humor you can include in your arsenal.

1) Double Meaning

- Gently toss the girl a tennis ball. After she catches it, say, "You're a great catch."

- "I'm on a see-food diet. I only eat the food I see."

- "You have big ears… just like Dumbo."

2) False Expectations

- You are with a friend at McDonald's.

    "You know what this place reminds me of… McDonald's"

    She expected you to say something thoughtful.

- You are speaking with a guest who just arrived at your home.

    "Thank you for coming over for dinner. If there is anything and I mean anything that could be done to make your visit more enjoyable, please don't hesitate to let Eric know."

    They expect you, not Eric, to host since they're at your home.

- You and your friend are wondering what the weather will be like tomorrow.

    "I'll bet you all the money in Calvin's wallet that it's not going to rain tomorrow."

    She expected you to bet your own money, not someone else's.

3) Freudian Slip

- "Jack, so where did you steal, I mean, buy this newspaper?"

- "Stuart, so how did you cheat, I mean, beat Linda at Scrabble?"

- "Willy, so who did you pay off, I mean, get help from?"

4) Good News-Bad News

- The good news is that I fixed your car. The bad news is that in the process I broke something else.

Peanut Butter & Jelly

- The good news is that she is unattached. The bad news is that you have a better chance of being hit by a meteorite.

- The good news is that your appetite is back. The bad news is all there is in the fridge is ketchup.

5) Ignorance

- "You're from Florida? That's awesome. So what state is that in?"

- "Yeah, we can go for French food tonight. I'm always up for some good French fries."

- Girl: Yeah, sometimes a girl's feelings are out of control.
  Guy: Wait, are you telling me that girls have emotions?

6) Implication

- "Since you're alive, I suppose the bank robbery went OK?"

  This implies that he robbed a bank when he didn't.

- "Collin, good to see you. So how was your experience in the state penitentiary?"

  This implies he was locked up in prison when he wasn't.

- "What planet did you say you're from again?"

  This implies that the person is from another planet.

7) Instigator

- Girl: How's your day?
  Guy: How about I'll tell you what you can handle?

- Girl: How do you feel about a guy dating an older girl?
  Guy: Well, it's hard for guys to find mature girls their age. We have to look up.

- Guy: Do we really need to play guys versus girls? Last time we played, it wasn't even close.

8) The Obvious

- When you and a friend are taking a hike through the woods, point to a tree and exclaim, "Hey, look it's a tree."

- On a clear sunny day, say to your friend, "Look, the sun's out."

- When you are on a boat, announce to all aboard, "Look, there's water all around us."

9) Sarcasm

   Say things in a monotone way as if you didn't care.

   - Girl: Are you coming to my graduation tomorrow?
     Guy: I guess so, there's nothing else to do.

   - Do you think being at your live concert will be as good as listening to it on my ipod?

   - Oh great. Another perfectly rainy day for a BBQ.

10) Self-Deprication

    - I'm a motivational speaker, though some people think I'm de-motivating.

    - Girls think I'm a loser. I think they're probably right.

    - I always end up losing all my bait when I go fishing. Either the fish are so smart they can get the bait without biting the hook or I suck. I hope the fish are smart.

11) Self-Praise

    - Girl: You said you had a secret. What is it?
      Guy: My weakness is kryptonite.

    - Some people mistaken me for Elvis, but I keep telling them I'm not as charming as he is. They think I'm lying.

    - I don't mean to sound prideful, but I think Deep Blue will have a hard time beating me at chess. You see, I don't play like Garry Kasparov or Bobby Fischer. I'm quite unpredictable.

12) Shocker

    - Guy to a girl: Can I get your contact info before all these other guys swarm all over ya?

    - Guy to a girl: Do you believe in love at first sight? I thought I'd ask

Peanut Butter & Jelly

since this is the first time we've ever seen each other.

- Guy to a girl: I can answer your question, but then I'd have to kill you. Do you still want to know?

13) Witty

- Guy 1: There should be a panic button on the subway.
  Guy 2: If there was, the trains would never move.

- Guy 1: Do you think people came to my birthday party with impure motives?
  Guy 2: I know I did. I came for the free food.

- Guy 1: Peggy gave me some cookies, but they're so hard to bite into. That's a strange way to show your interest in a guy.
  Guy 2: Maybe she doesn't like you. Ever think of that?

8) Just Do It

Many guys lack confidence and aren't too sure of themselves. Perhaps this may describe you. Before you despair, there's good news: confidence can be learned. Let me suggest my simple, one-step confidence boosting program…

Just Do It[12]

Don't think you'll become confident by simply reading books or listening to motivational speakers. You need to get out there, open your mouth, and talk to girls. There's just no other way around it. Be wary of analysis paralysis (thinking too much without doing anything about it).

Confidence must be developed. If you struggle with confidence, ask God to help you. Don't expect to become Mr. Confidence tomorrow without some trial and error. Along the way you'll get some cuts and bruises, but that's the only way you'll get better. Start small, then take bigger and bigger steps.

Try small talking with strangers. You can find them anywhere including at:

- BBQ's
- shops
- picnics
- bus stops
- coffee shops
- social events
- park benches
- grocery stores
- fitness classes

The possibilities are endless. Talking to strangers is more of a stretch out of your comfort zone than talking to your friends or family. And that's exactly what you want. By the way, if you mess up, chances are you will never see them again anyway. You have nothing to lose. To build confidence, venture out to the world of the unknown. It's time to leave the Shire, Frodo.[13]

Here are some sample conversation starters:

- "What time is it?"
- "That's a great accent. Where are you from?"
- "That's a great looking dog. What kind of dog is it?" (Use this only if she has a dog.)

---

12   Nike's slogan.

13   The ring-bearer in *The Lord of the Rings* whose mission was to leave his home, travel through unfamiliar lands in order to destroy the evil ring.

- "Cool yoga mat. How do you like your yoga class?"
- "How do you enjoy that book you're reading?"
- "I'm new to town. Can you recommend a good restaurant?"
- "That's a cool laptop. Would you recommend Apple?"
- "That's a real neat Paul Frank shirt. Where did you get it?"
- "Can you tell me how to get to Sesame Street?"

By the way, the last conversation starter was a joke. If you still don't get it, you're a little slow. Don't worry. God loves slow people, too.

If you struggle with confidence, set standards for yourself and force yourself to work on them. It's even better if you have an accountability partner to report back to. Effective accountability requires consequences for failure. For example, if you don't do what you agreed to within the agreed time (i.e. Call the girl you like by Friday or initiate three conversations with strangers in 48 hours…), then you owe $100 to your favorite charity or something like that.

Once in a while you meet an interesting girl out of nowhere. You might meet her at a friend's wedding, on a flight, while vacationing, at a party, or at a community service event. Hopeless romantics call this… serendipity.

ser·en·dip·i·ty (n) the art of making happy discoveries, or finding the unexpectedly pleasant by chance or sagacity[14]

If you meet such a girl, and you're not sure if your paths will ever cross again get her contact info. Really, all you need is an e-mail address to keep the ball rolling. Think of a way that would make her want to give you her e-mail. Throw out the right bait, otherwise, the fishies will not bite and you won't have anything to show mom.

Here are some examples:

- "Hannah, so you're into photography, huh? One of my friends is in that line of work, too. She's got a great website I think you would absolutely love. Let me send that link to you. Here's some paper. Maybe you can write down your e-mail for me."

---

14   www.serendipity3.com

- "Olivia, I'm so impressed you're into poetry, too. I'm working on a couple of poems. I should send them to you and see what you think. Do you have an e-mail?"

- "Brianna, I'm glad to meet someone new to town. Actually, I know quite a few good restaurants and dessert bars here you should totally check out. Let me e-mail you my top 10 list. What's your e-mail?"

The advantage of asking for an e-mail instead of a phone number is that it is less forward and upfront. Some girls take a while to warm up and a phone number may be too personal a thing for her to give away because she doesn't know you. With an e-mail, you can trade some e-mails back and forth and if you both hit it off, it'd be no problem to get a phone number and take it from there.

Other examples of goal setting may include:

- "I'm gonna call Teresa to see if she is getting over her flu."

- "I'm gonna invite Rebecca to hang out on Saturday night."

- "I'm gonna talk to Melody and ask how her art display went."

- "I'm gonna chat with Julie to see if she needs help with the reunion."

Goal setting starts with a decisive commitment of "I'm gonna…" Set weekly, if not daily goals. The more goals you set for yourself, the more progress you'll make, and the more confidence you'll have. Before you know it, talking to girls will be a no brainer and you won't dread asking girls out as much.

Confident guys have all endured numerous rejections in life, whether it be from girls or other avenues, and learned from their rejections. The key is not to view rejection as failure, but as a growing experience. Today's confident guys have all paid their dues.

Here is what my friend Christie Chong has to say about masculine initiative:

Asking a girl out or being vulnerable about your feelings is an act that is truly heroic and should be honored. It's something that shows a lot of bravery and sacrifice, and it is not easy. So when a guy takes initiative with a girl, this

Peanut Butter & Jelly

is what it tells her: that the guy deems her worthy enough for his risk. It tells her that she is worth the fight and is so special as to incite such motivation in him. In taking initiative, you do one of the greatest services to women—affirming their worthiness and honoring their choice to decide to be with you or not. That is the risk.[15]

You only get to live once. Don't let fishies go by without throwing out bait.

9) How to Ask a Girl Out

Let's be realistic. You're not going to hit a homerun the first time you swing a bat, so don't expect to hit a homerun with a girl either. In fact, chances are you will strike out numerous times before you hit even a single. So if a girl strikes you out, don't fret it. Keep swinging for them fences.

- **Ask Face to Face**

By asking face-to-face you can see the girl's body language and facial expression, which tells you how she feels. Her body language will not lie. If she's all smiles, that's a good sign. If she's all "What the?" that's not a good sign. If you're not good at reading body language, it's time to learn.

Yeah, you may misread a girl's body language from time to time, but that's OK. Hopefully, you'll get better with enough practice. Once you accurately

15   www.xanga.com/whatwomenwant

interpret a girl's body language along with her hints, the quality of your female friendships will dramatically improve.

- **Ask Through Writing**

Writing a note is another way to ask a girl out. This approach doesn't put her on the spot to come up with an answer right away, giving her time to think and process. This note could come in the form of an e-mail or instant message, or handwritten and given in person or snail mailed. If your handwriting sucks I give you permission to type and print it out. A girl would be quite impressed you went through all that effort to handwrite a note.

A simple note could be:

Lucy,

Let's get lemonade sometime. What do you say?

Signed,

Charlie Brown

- **Ask Through Calling**

Call her. To do this, get her phone number. You can get it from her facebook or one of her friends, but I recommend that you get it directly from her. A girl might creep out that you got her number without her giving it.

If you can't get her phone number directly, but can get it indirectly that's better than nothing. However, once she picks up your call let her know how you got her number so she doesn't think you are a sketchy guy.

There are two ways to get a girl's phone number.

- Direct approach—"Can I call you sometime?"

Depending on how well you hit it off with the girl, this can be appropriate. The down side is sometimes it may be too strong of a move and hence you might scare the girl away. Believe it or not, girls can get scared off. But if the girl is interested in you, you'll score big and impress her with your confidence.

- Indirect approach—This approach is safer and less risky.

Here are some examples:

- "Say, Jennifer, can I call you about the homework? Maybe I should get your number?"
- "Denise, it's getting late. I'll call you later to make sure you get home OK. Is that cool?"
- "Terri, didn't you organize the picnic last year? Actually, I'm in charge this year. I should call you to get some ideas. What's a good number to reach you?"

For starters, I'd recommend the indirect approach so that you have a legitimate excuse to call her (i.e. homework, getting home OK, picnic …).

How to Turn a Conversation

Here's an example of how you can get to know a girl better through one of these calls.

Girl: Hello?

Guy: Hey, it's me. Did you get home, OK?

Girl: Yeah, thanks for calling. I appreciate it.

Guy: Yeah, don't mention it. That's why guys exist, right?

Girl: That's funny. (Anytime you can get a girl to laugh, you're on your way.)

Guy: Say, how did you like the musical tonight? (Notice how the guy turns the conversation to small talking about other things. A smart and smooth transition—Way to go.)

Get a sense of how receptive a girl is through a simple phone conversation. If she is warm toward you, perhaps you should ask her out.

Voice Mail

Ideally, when you call, the girl picks up. If you get her voice mail the first or second time, it's better not to leave a message. Hopefully, when you call a couple of hours later she'll pick up. If you still get her voice mail, then go ahead and leave her a message.

Whatever you do, don't constantly call her every five minutes and not leave a voice mail. The girl will freak out thinking, "Why does Bob keep calling and not leaving a voice mail? How creepy." Even if you've blocked your caller ID, she might think, "Who's this person who keeps calling me every five minutes? It must be Bob. What a shady guy."

If you get her voice mail, don't leave a message asking her out. Simply ask her to call you back at her convenience. Here is a simple voice message you can leave:

"Hello Dorothy. This is Stevie from the New Year's party. My number is: (Say your phone number). Would you call me when you get a chance? Thanks. Again my number is: (Say your phone number). Take care. Bye."

Leave your phone number on the voicemail twice; at the beginning and the end to insure she doesn't mishear.

If she doesn't return your call within 48 hours, call her again. If you get her voice mail, leave her another message. Whatever you do, don't say: "How come you're not calling me back? Are you avoiding me?" If she still doesn't return your call, just leave it at that. I know it's hard, but it's counterproductive to think about why she's not calling you back.

The next time you see the girl you could ask, "Hey Laura. I've been trying to get a hold of you. Get my voice mail?" If she says no, then go ahead and ask her out. If she says yes and says she's been too busy to call you back, that's a clue she's not interested so give her space. An exception is if she says something like, "Oh yeah, I got your calls. I'm sorry for not returning them. I was out of town. I meant to do so later on today."

Free tip: The sooner a girl returns your call the more interested she is in you.

- Never Ask Through Someone Else

Remember junior high? You told your friend Robert about your secret crush on Linda and to ask Linda if she likes you. Why didn't you ask her yourself? Well, it all comes down to face and guts. You want to score without getting rejected. If Robert reported to you that Linda told you to "Take a hike!" you would go to Linda and tell her that Robert was just being stupid and messin' around.

Guess what? You're not in junior high any more. Surprised? Always directly go to the girl you're interested in without any middleman, including her good friends. It's OK to talk to her friends about what they think of the two of you hitting it off, but don't use them to relay the message. Don't be chicken dung.

In war, you fire missiles for a direct hit. You shoot straight for the target. It's no different when you're going for the girl. Going through someone else means you really aren't man enough to accept the consequences of being turned down. That's wimpy. Be bold, Braveheart![16]

I'm not saying you shouldn't use your friends to help you get a date with this girl. Not at all. In fact, it might not be a bad idea for you to ask your friends for some help and to put in a good word for you. Since girls will be more or less open to dating a guy based on his reputation, it will help if the people she knew thought highly of you.

Of course, if there is nothing good about you, don't tell them to lie and make something up, but I'm assuming if you've gotten this far in the book, then you're, at least, a half-way decent guy. I hope I'm right. Don't let me down.

Group Things

For starters, organize some group things and invite the girl to tag along. In fact, she'd probably feel even more comfortable if she could bring a friend or two—so invite her to invite her friends.

In one-on-one settings, there may be pressure to keep the conversation rolling when you hit speed bumps. The group setting puts you both more at ease. You can talk when you have something to say or just listen to others.

Invite friends to group outings who can help you get to know the girl better. For example, if you're going to a baseball game ask your friends, "Hey guys, I'm interested in Betty. Since we have four seats together, would it be cool if you guys orchestrate things so I can sit next to Betty? I'll tell you what. If you guys help me out, I'll buy you garlic fries. Do we have a deal? By the way, don't make it obvious I'm trying to sit next to Betty, OK?"

Do you have a wingman, a friend whose life mission is to help you find the perfect match and set you up? If your wingman personally knows the girl you like, encourage him to help you. He can say to the girl, "I'm having a backyard BBQ this weekend, wanna come?"

---

16   William Wallace was a valiant Scottish soldier who fought the British in a Mel Gibson movie.

Hopefully, the girl comes and you just happen to be there, too. This would make for a casual time of getting to know each other. See how your wingman can help you? If you and the girl hit it off, then ask her out to group things or one-on-one dates. Go get her, Tiger!

Ways to Get a Date

Let me share a couple of ways to get a date where you can't lose.

- Return the Favor

Ask the girl to help you with something. It could be picking you up from the airport, sewing a loose button on your shirt, running an errand for you, dropping you off at work because your car broke down, and so on.

Afterwards say something like, "Julie, thanks for helping me out the other day. Lemme take you out for dinner to return the favor." Initially, she will probably say something like, "Oh no. It's OK. Don't worry about it. It's no big thing."

Respond with "Actually, I would like to. It's the least I could do." She may insist, "Really. It's not a biggie." If so, say something like, "Julie, really, I'd like to take you out. I'd feel so much better if I can. At the very least, would you let me take you out so I can feel better?"

- Bet Her

Tell the girl, "Lisa, I bet you I can beat you at bowling." Lisa may say, "You're on, mister." Respond with "OK. The loser makes a home-cooked meal for the winner. Are we still on? You can back out if you're chicken." Hopefully, your dare will entice her to accept the bet.

If you suspect the girl can't cook, try this, "Joanne, I bet you I could beat you at Connect Four.[17] You up for the challenge?" She may say, "I'm not scared of you. What's on the line?" Respond with, "Loser buys. Are you ready to buy?"

These are great bets because either way, whether you win or lose, you'll get a date with the girl. It's a win-win situation. This also gives you an opportunity to get to know her. An easy way to increase the number of dates is to keep losing and saying, "Double or nothing." If your strategy is to lose, don't make it obvious. With the double or nothing approach, you can easily owe her many meals.

---

17   The object of this game is to connect four checkers in a row first. I had a 50 game winning streak at one point. Not bad, huh? Of course, it was against my 95 year old granny whom I taught to play, but still.

High vs. Low Maintenance Girls

If she's a high maintenance girl, take her to the San Diego Zoo[18] or something like that. If she thinks she's too cool for the lions and tigers and bears, that's a sign that she's not a keeper.

If you're low on cash, find out when the public museums or exhibits are free and go then. When you get there act surprised. "What do you know? It's free today. Guess I don't need to shell out my hard earned money. Shucks."

Remember to say that so she won't think you're cheap. Whew. Saved you some $[19] there, didn't I? Actually, I just saved you more than the cost of this book, so your investment paid off.

If she's low maintenance, do something simple like ask her out to In-N-Out[20] and munch on some fries together. If she's super-low maintenance, take her to the most ghetto, hole-in-the-wall, ambiance deficient food joint you can find. If she still likes you after that, she's a keeper.

Free tip: If the girl is willing to go out with you even if you are in debt it's a sure sign of true love. You can take that to the bank.

When you ask her out, make sure the occasion is something both of you enjoy. For example, if the girl is really into entertainment wrestling (i.e. watching The Rock body-slam "Stone Cold" Steve Austin[21]), but you, being a civilized gentleman, think that's barbaric, perhaps you can compromise and ask her out to watch something less caveman-like such as *Disney on Ice*.

Free tip: If she thinks you're a wimp for not enjoying raw and senseless violence like entertainment wrestling find another girl to ask out.

---

18   A zoo in San Diego.
19   Symbol for cash, which Australians call buckaroos. I'm just kidding. Buckaroos just sound cool.
20   My favorite fast food burger joint known for fresh ingredients and a clean, sparkling, and fun environment. Ask for free bumper stickers.
21   WWE (World Wrestling Entertainment) superstars. I watched these wrestling matches religiously when I was in elementary school. I'd pinned my little brother down with full nelsons (AKA double headlocks). Then, he'd tell Mama and I'd get a whooping.

Peanut Butter & Jelly

10) Getting to Know Her

Let's hear what Kate Chan has to say about getting to know someone you're romantically interested in:

Suppose you got digits from an SGI (someone of great interest), and even landed a date with her. Your first date went fairly smoothly—she laughed at your jokes, you didn't spill anything on her, and you got her home in one piece. Good job.

Now comes the hard part. You may be asking yourself, how often should I call her? How often should I ask her out on a date? How much contact is too much? How much is too little?

On the one hand, you don't want to annoy her, crowd her space, or scare her off. On the other hand, you don't want to seem too disinterested, or drag out the getting-to-know-you period too long because, frankly, you have a life, too.

Basically, how frequently you ask her out will depend on several factors: how interested you are in her, how interested she is in you, and how many other guys are pursuing her at the moment.

Let the girl set the pace. This you can usually gauge by her cues. For example, if she always calls you back right away, and readily accepts your dates without much hesitation, or without needing to think about it, then this is usually a good sign. You can keep the frequency of dates at about once a week, and phone calls at about twice a week to start off. If when you call her, she somehow always finds a way to prolong the conversation and you end up talking for hours on end, or on your dates, she doesn't seem all too eager to go home at the end of it, this is usually a very good sign. After a couple of successful dates of about once a week, you can up the ante as she feels comfortable.

However, if the girl does not return your calls right away or after a couple of days, or accepts your dates, then try to extend the intervals between the dates, saying, "Maybe not this week, how about next week, or two weeks from now?" This probably means that she is somewhat interested, but perhaps not super-duper interested. (Or perhaps she has other guys pursuing her at the same time, and if she were to go out with each of them once a week, that would pretty much book up all her nights, which would not only be exhausting, but not be very practical for her.) If this were the case, I would lower the frequency of contact to her comfort level, basically let her set the pace. Perhaps you would only see each other only once every other week, or even less, depending on her level of interest.

However, if the pace that the girl has set is way too slow for you, or if your interest level in her is not enough for you to continue the pursuit at such a pace, don't feel obliged to keep pursuing if you don't feel it's worth it. You can either see other people in the meantime, or stop calling her or asking her out altogether. If the girl was not that super interested in you in the first place, she would probably not mind it too much if you suddenly disappeared off her radar.

Part 3: Understanding Girl-Talk

11) What She Really Means

Let's hear what Kate Chan says about what a girl means by her words:

Response: *"No, thanks."*
Translation: Not interested.

Response: *Never writes or calls back...*
Translation: Not interested. Give her space.
Slight possibility: *She was in fact busy and simply forgot to write back... you might want to ask her a second time. If you still get no response, give her space. She's most likely not interested.*

Response: *Makes a lot of excuses (sometimes really lame ones, e.g. "I'm washing my hair") without trying to reschedule, or suggesting alternate dates.*
Translation: Not interested. After two or three excuses that are kind of lame, without any effort on her part to reschedule, it's time to get the hint and move on...

Response: *"Uhhh.... sure... maybe....(with lots of hesitation)."*
Translation: Probably leaning more towards: Okay with being friends, but probably not interested in being more—although it's not necessarily a total rule out.

(Note: This is one of the more ambiguous responses. Her hesitation may be a subtle hint to you that she is not interested in that way. But since you have not made your intentions explicit, she does not want to be presumptuous by assuming you have any such intentions. Or she is not that interested, but is willing to give you at least a chance by going out on a date with you. Or she is just really freaked out by being asked out on a date. I would suggest still trying... Most likely the girl will let you know her level of interest soon enough... either with an explicit DTR[22] or with one of the other responses.)

---

22   Define the relationship. See Book 1, Chapter 17.

Peanut Butter & Jelly

Response: *"Okay..." "Sure." (Without much hesitation.)*
Translation: Open to getting to know you better. Possibly interested. (Need more info to determine this.)

Response: *"I would love to, but I'm busy... Maybe next time." "I can't this week... (legitimate excuse), how about next week?"*
Translation: Interested, or least open to getting to know you better, but just happens to be busy. This is a good sign, keep trying...

Response: *"Yeah, that would be great..." (Positive response.) "Yeah, let's do (such and such)..." (Makes suggestions on what to do, where to go... Or even invites you to do things.)*
Translation: Definitely interested in getting to know you better...

Disclaimer: This is a general guideline that I came up with based on my own experiences and may not apply to all girls.

12) Walking on Eggs

Sometimes asking a girl out is like walking on eggs. It's delicate and uncomfortable. For instance, a girl may be so shocked you asked her out for a date that she might ask any of the following:

- "Did you have something you want to talk about?"
- "Is there some kind of occasion I should know about?"

Please don't be offended if a girl asks this. Just respond with something short and simple, "Debbie, you're a real neat girl. I'd like to get to know you better."

If she is not completely dense, she'll understand what you are saying. Whatever you do, don't spill all your beans and say, "Well, Debbie, I want to see if you would be the right person for me to start a huge, and I mean huge, family together with. Are you the love of my life? My Juliet?[23] Will you be the one who takes my breath away?"

Sometimes, a girl may say something like "I'm really busy these days." 99% of the time, this is her way of delaying a no response. She just wants to better collect her thoughts before turning you down. If a girl is interested in getting to know you better, no matter how busy she may be, she will never say, "I'm busy" without, at least rescheduling, "I'd like to hang out with you. This Saturday won't work, but how about Sunday?"

Free tip: Many girls will only understand a guy asking her out to be a romantic gesture so be warned. Depending on whether a girl likes a guy to be upfront early or not, it may or may not be best for you to express all your feelings. Each girl is different so you need to strike at an appropriate time.

Free tip: When you ask a girl out and she looks uncomfortable, consider backing out of the date immediately by saying, "Actually, let's just pretend I didn't say anything. OK. I have to go now. Bye." You've just spared a significant amount of awkwardness between the two of you.

When You Don't Get a Response

Sometimes when you ask a girl out, she might say, "Let me get back to you," but never will. She's just more comfortable not telling you no. Any girl who is interested will not forget to get back to you.

Just because a girl says, "Let me get back to you" doesn't mean that she necessarily will. Here are two possible outcomes:

---

[23] A reference to William Shakespeare's best-known novel *Romeo & Juliet*.

- She pretends nothing happened.

She pretends you never asked her out in the first place. She'll talk to you and treat you as if nothing happened while all the time you're left hangin' and waiting for her response, which never comes.

- She gives you the silent treatment.

She starts distancing herself from you both emotionally and conversationally. Her interactions with you may be brief and not engaging. She may not smile at you the way she used to. The girl may not look you in the eye the way she once did. She may not ask you how you are doing or if she does it's more so out of courtesy than personal interest. In some cases, the girl may straight up avoid you.

Here are two possible reasons why she reacts this way:

- You creep her out. It's the freak factor. Perhaps she's had bad experiences. If a girl is freaked out, stop asking her out, lest she'd feel even more freaked out by you.
- She thinks you are romantically interested in her, doesn't feel the same way about you, and doesn't want to complicate the friendship further by going out with you.

If a girl doesn't give you a response, she is a conflict avoider. This may indicate a shortcoming in her character. If she avoids things as small as getting back to you with a response, chances are she will avoid dealing with other issues in her life and in the lives of others. Sure, this can change over time, but nevertheless, this is a yellow flag, a warning.

If you don't get a response from a girl, I feel your pain, man. Should you follow up with the girl to clear the air? In most cases, you should. A girl needs to learn how to communicate and resolve conflicts. Difficulty in this area will affect the quality of her relationships and future marriage.

However, if a girl is particularly sensitive, you may not want to talk to her about this. Moreover, you need to decide what to say, if anything, and how to say it. Regardless of what you decide to do, give the girl plenty of space.

If you follow up with the girl, don't spill all your beans. Start with something brief. If she wants to talk about it some more, go ahead and hash it out. Be careful not to sound like you're attacking her in any way like "I can't believe you didn't even respond."

Instead say something like, "Brenda, I could be wrong about this, but it seems like the last few weeks something has been bothering you. I'm just wondering if I said or did anything that made you uneasy. Is there anything we need to talk about?"

If she isn't open to talking to you about this after you bring it up, consider dropping the subject altogether.

Part 4: When She Gives You a Lemon

13) When She Says No

Don't be too surprised if a girl says no. Apart from God, you suck. Why wouldn't a girl say no to you? If a girl says yes, hopefully, it's because she sees your love for Jesus. Such a girl is extremely precious, a rare find. If you have such a girl in your life, consider her a wonderful blessing from God.

Don't ever think you are worthy of a girl's love. You never are, just as you are never worthy of God's love. Once you think you are worthy of her love, you run the risk of treating her like no special thing. It's like taking God's grace for granted.

When you don't feel worthy of a girl's love, you'll treat her more like the treasure she truly is. God didn't need to create Eve for Adam. It was a bonus. And a great bonus it was. Don't ever think you deserve anything.

When you want to get to know a girl better, you get excited. But if the girl is not interested or not that interested in you, you'll get disappointed and hurt. And you know what? That's OK. That's the risk you take when you ask a girl out.

Keep in mind that by asking her out, it may forever change your friendship. It is not uncommon to lose a friendship. Some girls may distance themselves from you after you ask them out because they don't feel comfortable about where the friendship may be going.

If the girl turns you down say something like, "Suzy, thanks for considering it. You're my good friend. I wish you the best." This makes a girl feel relaxed and at ease. If you don't say this, the girl may feel bad for saying no to you. Allow her to freely choose to say no to you without jeopardizing the friendship. Lesser guys will not accept no for an answer. They are plentiful in this world. Don't become another.

Maintain your composure after a girl says no. Smile and talk to her as if you were in no way affected by her rejection so she won't feel guilty for turning you down. Never show or tell her how hurt you feel. Not only is that unnecessary for her to know, it's best for her not to know. If you want to cry in private, go ahead.

Free tip: Some guys may ask a girl to give a reason or two why she doesn't want to go out. Keep in mind that she doesn't have to give any reason at all. Just like in a department store, it's nice to be able to return merchandise with no questions asked. Some girls don't like being asked the question "Why not?" so be sensitive to this.

Does No Mean No?

When a girl says no does she mean never? Not necessarily, but you must honor her wish. A girl usually says no because she is either not interested in you or unsure about you. If you asked her out after knowing her for five days and she said no, she is not necessarily dismissing the possibility of getting to know you for life. Six months from now she may know you better and be open.

If you have a real neat godly girl in mind, you might not want to just drop all your hopes of getting to know her just because she said no. Who knows? Sometime in the future she may be interested in you. Girls take longer to warm up to guys than vice versa.

Peanut Butter & Jelly

Even if the girl says no, it's not a failure. Don't see it that way. You've just communicated to the girl: "I think that you are wonderful and worth sticking my neck out for. If you haven't thought of me as an option, please do."

14) Pursuing the Girl

If you still want to pursue this girl after she turned you down, you could, but I wouldn't recommend going too far. Figure out where she is drawing the line in the sand and don't step across it. Take baby steps and if she's warm toward you, aim for bigger steps, but start small, OK?

One thing you could do to keep things rolling is to organize some group things to get to know her better. Try any of the following:

- serving those in need
- listening to a musical
- playing miniature golf
- walking around the zoo
- watching a baseball game
- helping out at a soup kitchen

There are many group things you can do, but be warned. You may be further disappointed and hurt if she doesn't show up to them. But it's OK. You're a man. You can handle it, right?

For example, let's say you organize a baseball game outing, only to find out everybody, but the girl you organized it for, is coming. Doesn't that suck? You spent so much time researching the baseball schedule, e-mailing everybody, getting your hopes up and the girl doesn't even respond to your e-mail invitation.

You're probably asking, "Should I still pursue this girl?" Let me turn the tables back to you and have you ask yourself, "Is this girl worth my effort and all the possible pains and disappointments involved?" A godly girl is indeed a rare find. If the girl is worth your effort, you'd be foolish not to give it a good try.

Christie Chong has this to say to guys about being patient with girls:

Guys need to understand that it does take time for our heads to catch up with our hearts. Please be patient and persistent (up to a point). Since committing to you is such a huge emotional investment and risk for us, it is a heavy decision that needs to be weighed. The heart is there, but the mind needs time to catch up and validate the feelings. Don't take advantage of the emotionally charged state of her heart in your favor, but respect the girl enough to wait for every part of her (including her mind and will) to truly and purely want to be with you. Once that decision is made, the girl will go all out and give her all to you. Well worth the wait.[24]

15) Un-Breaking Your Heart

When a girl says no, she'll break your heart. Yes, contrary to popular belief, guys have feelings, too. You may feel bitter, angry, mad, depressed, and so on. It's not uncommon to want to hurt her back and hope something bad happens to her so she realizes how much she needs you. Just because you naturally feel this way doesn't make it right.

Don't pretend you don't have these feelings and just sweep them under the mat. Instead, tell God how you feel and ask Him to help you. Grieving over a broken heart is OK. The psalmists did it. Take all the time you need to clear your system. Just don't stay there forever.

---

24   www.xanga.com/whatwomenwant

Peanut Butter & Jelly

Elisabeth Elliot, an insightful writer, once said, *"The love life of a Christian is a crucial battleground. There, if nowhere else, it will be determined as to who is Lord: the world, the self and the devil, or the Lord Christ."*[25]

How true. Your love life is dearest of all human relationships. Just as Abraham offered Isaac, so you must be willing to give up what you hold most dear. If you are not, you are making her an idol. Your willingness or lack thereof to give her up indicates your heart's condition before the Lord.

If the thought of seeing her brings you pain and disappointment, tell God about it. The turmoil of unreciprocated love has plunged many guys into some deep soul searching, but there is hope in the midst of it all.

Here is one of my favorite poems to read when I'm struggling:

I look up to the mountains; does my strength come from mountains?
  No, my strength comes from God,
    who made heaven, and earth, and mountains.

He won't let you stumble,
  your Guardian God won't fall asleep.
Not on your life! Israel's
  Guardian will never doze or sleep.

God's your Guardian,
  right at your side to protect you—
Shielding you from sunstroke,
  sheltering you from moonstroke.

GOD guards you from every evil,
  he guards your very life.
He guards you when you leave and when you return,
  he guards you now, he guards you always.[26]

Do not let these feelings of hurt and disappointment consume you. Know what I mean? Instead, control your mind. Don't be consumed with being hurt, but be consumed with how you can still love and serve this sister-in-Christ who just broke your heart. Think about how to bless her as difficult as that may be.

---

25   Elisabeth Elliot, *Passion and Purity*, P. 12
26   Psalm 121

Be careful how far you go to love and serve her though. For example, if she doesn't want you to e-mail her anymore or as frequently as before, then don't. If she doesn't want to talk to you, then back off and give her space. Seek to bless her, but only to the degree she allows you to. Meanwhile keep yourself busy with meeting the needs of people around you. Whatever you do, don't wallow in self-pity. This helps no one.

16) Life Goes On

After my first big heartbreak over Candy, my friend David told me, "Mike, life goes on." At that time, I couldn't disagree with him more. I was so depressed I even lost my appetite for food. I thought this was the end of me, but in due time I did recover. As a survivor, let me tell you that even if you suffer heartbreaks, life still goes on.

The emotional pain of unreciprocated love makes it hard for the guy and girl to still be friends. The quickest way to get over a person is to not see the person anymore. For example, if you both go to the same church[27] consider going somewhere else to give each other a break from seeing one another.

The girl may not outright admit just how difficult it is to see you around, but she will probably appreciate not seeing you much, at least for a while. This helps put her mind to rest and not think any of the following:

- "Does he feel comfortable with me?"
- "What if there's an awkward silence between us?"
- "What should I say to him when I see him at church?"

Your disappearance expedites the healing process. But before you disappear tell her you are cool with her and wish her the best. Ideally, say this right after she turns you down.

To make your transition smooth continue going to the same church for about 30 more days before disappearing. During this time if you see her be sure to make eye contact and at least speak with her briefly. This way she won't think you are purposely trying to avoid her. This is an extremely sensitive time in your friendship. If you don't make eye contact, even though you might not be purposefully avoiding her, she may take it to mean you are and feel guilty.

---

27   Or any place you are bound to bump into her. For the sake of simplicity, we'll just call it church.

Peanut Butter & Jelly

If you disappear right after she says no, she may connect the dots in her head and think you left because she turned you down and feel guilty about it. After 30 days, she may not associate your leaving with her telling you no and that's exactly what you want. If she asks you why you don't go to church anymore, say something positive, "My friend Jack thought I should check out his ministry, so I did, liked it, and have been there since."

Do not tell her you are going to another church because you're too hurt to see her. Don't lie, but at the same time, use wisdom in what you say and how you say things. Do not make her feel guilty in any way.

Part 5: When She Says Yes

17) DTR: Define the Relationship

If after a few dates you don't feel the Lord is leading in this relationship, you could just stop there or not hang out with her as much. However, if you think she needs more of a verbal explanation of what is going on between the two of you, politely tell her, "Let's just be friends."

But suppose you get a few dates with this neat girl and you feel God wants you to pursue her even further. What's the next step? Great question. It's time to DTR (Define the relationship).

A DTR is when you state your romantic intentions more clearly and ask her how she feels about exploring a romance together. You don't have to do this on the second date, but as a general rule, do this by the fifth one-on-one date at the latest.

To gauge her interest, say something like, "Mimi, you're a real neat girl. I'd like to get to know you even better. I was wondering how you feel about me?"[28]

If she reciprocates, go out on a few more dates or talk about dating exclusively. Assuming God's leading in this and her parents' blessings you can talk about your life direction in further detail. Be upfront about things. For example, if you are planning to become a martyr, which may mean that she'll be a widow and single parent, make sure she knows that. Help her make an informed decision.

If you DTR, encourage her do some heavy duty contemplation. Don't just tell her the upsides of dating you, but the downsides, too. Why? Well, it keeps it real. You don't want to paint a picture in her mind that the rest of her life with you is going to be a magic carpet ride. Why not? Well, it's unrealistic… unless your name is Aladdin.[29]

Good luck, guys.

---

[28] A risk-free way to DTR is to ask her, "Mimi, if I had a twin brother who was like me in every way: personality, looks, intelligence, charm, career, athleticism, and so on, would you be interested in dating him?" If she says yes, she's open to dating you. This should be a slam dunk. If she says no, that's OK. She didn't turn you down, but your imaginary twin brother down. Side note: If you actually have a twin brother, you might not want to use this.

[29] A reference to Disney's *Aladdin*, a commoner, who along with his mischievous monkey Abu, wins the heart of Princess Jasmine through singing *A Whole New World* while carpet flying through the enchanted city. Aladdin sets a standard that's hard to beat.

Mike Toy & Audrey Jung

Book 2
How to Kiss the Right Frog
—For Girls Only

Guys are lucky in that they don't have to go around kissing frogs to find true love. Ick.

But just as guys have things to mull over and work on when relating to the opposite sex, girls have certain things to consider, too.

Here are some things girls might want to think about.

1) Loving God

Do you love God?

Would you praise God even if He never brings that special someone into your life? Is your love for Him conditional or is it something nothing can put asunder? Is there a price to your obedience? Of course, no one is perfect when it comes to loving God, but is that a growing desire in your life?

Often times, girls ask, "So where are all the godly guys?" Godly guys in this world are few, but godly girls are rare too. Complaining about how guys are not confident, spiritual, or competent is easy to do, but are you asking the

Peanut Butter & Jelly

hard questions of yourself? Only a girl who is willing to put God first and foremost in her life is ready to date.

- Do you earnestly desire to follow God?
- Are you actively serving people who cannot repay?
- Are you belittling your brothers-in-Christ or building them up?
- Are you praying for them?
- How are you actively encouraging them?
- Are you willing to pay any price to have the will of God done in your life?

If this is your desire, here is a simple prayer you can say:

Lord,

I want to follow you with my whole heart. Help me make you the love of my life.

Amen.

2) Don't Read Into Things

I once remember a girl "reading" too much. Amy invited me to a group ice skating outing. Something came up the night before so I told her I couldn't make it. I found out later she took that to mean I wasn't comfortable hanging out with her, which was not true at all. She was so distraught by my cancellation that a week later she pulled a DTR.[30]

Obviously, I was not ready for a DTR (this was my first one) and boy was that confusing. Though things never panned out for Amy and me, I learned a valuable lesson. Don't read into somebody's actions or words too much, especially if you're not intuitive. You can end up misinterpreting things altogether.

If you are unsure what a guy's intentions are, it may not be a good idea to ask him on the spot, especially if it is the first date. "Excuse me, Bob, do you want to get to know me better just as a friend or more than a friend?" This puts the guy in a tight spot and can scare a guy off. It's totally possible for him not to know his own intentions.

Just because a guy asks you out doesn't necessarily mean he is romantically interested in you. The guy is not getting on his knees and asking you to marry him on the spot, you know? Don't read into things too much. Some guys will ask you out just to get to know you better.

The bottom line is that he is interested in you for whatever reason. If you're not up for it, let him down nicely. Reciprocating interest when you have none makes things more complicated in the long run. Too many girls are in unhealthy relationships with guys today simply because they didn't cut things off early in the relationship and ended up becoming emotionally attached. That's exactly how a great girl ends up with a loser. Many guys out there know how to prey on emotionally vulnerable girls. Don't you become their victim.

3) How to Win a Guy's Attention

Some say that a way to a guy's heart is through his stomach. For those of you who are a little slow, what this means is that a guy cherishes a girl who can make him tasty food. While this is certainly true, there are at least two other factors that significantly affect the equation also, namely respect and loyalty.

---

30   Define the relationship. See Book 1, Chapter 17. You weren't supposed to read Book 1 because it was for guys only, but just so I don't have to explain DTR again, I'll let this one slide. Keep this between you and me.

Peanut Butter & Jelly

Respect

Let's look at respect first.

"Each wife is to honor her husband."[31]

Love to a girl is respect to a guy. Few guys can resist a girl who respects him. If you want to win a guy's attention, then R-E-S-P-E-C-T is a must.

Respect is manifested in many ways. Here are some examples:

- Speak highly of him to others

    "Randy definitely has a creative mind. Don't you think?"

- Speak highly of him to him

    "Tom, your knowledge of TVs is quite amazing."

- Value his thoughts and opinions

    "John, should I get red bean soup or green tea ice cream?"

- Appreciate his advice and counsel

    "Wilson, thanks for helping me with my Mandarin."

- Defer to him in decision-making

    "Gilbert, why don't you decide what my car needs and I'll go with it."

- Don't criticize him

    "That was incredibly dumb."

- Don't nag or complain

    "C'mon, I can't believe you forgot."

Guys can feel disrespected over what you consider trivial things. Here is an example:

When a guy is driving a girl around and is lost, he might feel attacked if you ask, "Should you ask a gas station dude? You're obviously lost." Have you ever wondered why? Obviously, respect is tied into this because he wants the

---

31   Ephesians 5:33

girl to trust him and not think he is incompetent. He wants to prove that he is man enough to get them where they need to go.

Guys like being the man. They like coming through for others. For example, if you need help buying a new TV, fixing a computer problem, servicing your car, or using power tools, ask a guy. This affirms him being a man.

Loyalty

Now, let's talk about loyalty.

Loyalty defined: An unwavering commitment to stick by someone through good times and bad.

Did you ever wonder why God created man's best friend before he created Eve? I'm talking about a dog. Well, that's cuz a dog is loyal. A dog is not going to run away from home or ditch his master. Nope. A dog is loyal to the very end.

Side Note: Don't get me wrong. I'm not a dog expert by any stretch of the imagination. In fact, I never had a dog. I think it's cuz I grew up in a Chinese family and it just doesn't make sense to have another mouth to feed. If you've never had a dog either, there's a good chance you're Chinese also.

When a guy is lucky enough to meet a loyal girl, it's a beautiful thing. He knows that she's got his back. He knows that she isn't going to abandon him when the going gets tough. He knows she isn't going to ditch him for greener grass. Such a girl is a precious find. It brings something special out of a guy. It makes him willing to go the extra mile for her.

Respect and loyalty are keys to a man's heart. If you're a girl, you'll do well to have these under your belt.

4) How to Make Yourself Approachable

Throwing hints to a guy makes it much easier for him to pursue you. If you don't throw hints, he might get the idea that you are not interested in him and might not pursue you. Here are some ideas:

Body Language

1) Be yourself. Don't try to impress him. Just be who God made you.

2) Smile a lot especially when you are with him.

3) Make great eye contact. This shows him that you value what he has to say; it also shows confidence. **The First Time**

4) When meeting a guy, be the first to introduce yourself. You can even be creative. "So, what's a stranger like you doing here?"

5) Ask him for his business card, then offer him yours even if he doesn't ask for it. Write your cell phone number on it.

6) After exchanging cards, say, "Cool. We should chill sometime."

7) In subsequent meetings, take the initiative to approach him and say hello.

Humor

8) Talk to him. This sounds ridiculously obvious, but sometimes a girl can get cold feet and disengage.

9) Laugh at his jokes even if they aren't that funny. Try to laugh a little bit or at the very least, laugh at his efforts to be funny. A guy feels good if he can make someone laugh. Whatever you do, do not ask him, "Was that a joke?" unless you can play it off.

10) If you have a sense of humor, use it. "Did you hear about that chicken joke? It's so funny. I should tell you…" You can tease him. "So Hotshot, what's the profound thought of the day?" "So, Wonderboy, save any lives lately?"

E-mail

11) When a guy e-mails you, e-mail him right back.

12) When you e-mail, sound as if receiving his e-mail made your day. "Gosh, Mike. I'm so glad to hear from you" or "Thanks so much for that encouraging word. It gave me a lift today."

13) When you e-mail, it should be longer than two or three lines. You can share a little bit about how your day or week is going.

14) Whenever you e-mail, ask him "So how are you doing?" or if you e-mail frequently you can comically ask, "So what did you do the last 24 hours?"

15) If you've promised to e-mail or contact him about something (i.e. more information on an event or introducing him to a friend…), do so as soon as possible.

Food

16) Bake some cookies or brownies and drop them off to him.

The Date

17) When a guy asks you out to a date or group outing, sound interested. "Yeah, sure. I'd love to go. Thanks for asking."

18) When a guy asks you out to a date or group outing and you can't make it, be sure to schedule an alternate time or ask him to let you know about other happenings again. "Oh, I'd love to go hiking. Can't make it this weekend, but let me know if you do it again sometime. I'd love to tag along." If you just say, "No, I can't go" and nothing further, he might get the impression that you are not interested in him.

19) After a date or group outing, express how much you enjoyed spending time together. "Thanks Mike. That was awesome. I had a great time. We should do this again."

Offer and Ask for Help

20) If he's from out of town, offer to show him around your city.

21) Ask him to help you entertain out-of-town guests. "My cousin from Beijing is coming to town. Wanna show him around town with me?"

Conversating[32]

22) When you hang out with your friends, invite him, "It'd be totally cool if you could come." Sound excited. Include him on your Evite© list.

23) Ask his friends about him. Eventually, word will get back to him that you asked. "Say guys, have you hung out with Mike lately?" or "Gosh, so what's Mike been up to?"

---

32   I think I just made up yet another word. You should try it. You might like it.

Peanut Butter & Jelly

24) Praise him. "Gosh, that's a nice jacket. Where'd you get it?" "Man, that was a killer casserole. How'd you make it?" "You sure know a lot about trivial things. You'd do great on Jeopardy."

25) Show interest in the things that interest him. "So, Mike, what are your latest thoughts on dating?" "So how did that miniature golf tournament go?" "Tell me all about your duck hunting trip."

26) Don't keep talking about certain guys too much otherwise he might think you're interested in them. To discourage him from thinking so you can say something like, "Elmer and I have been *friends* since high school." Emphasize the word *friends* when you say it so the guy you're interested in won't think that you and Elmer are an item.

27) If he misses a function, let him know that you noticed. "So where did you disappear to last Saturday?"

5) Right Place at the Right Time

> HEY. I ALWAYS BUMP INTO YOU AT THE PUNCH TABLE.
>
> I GUESS SIMPLE, I MEAN, GREAT MINDS THINK ALIKE.

Kate Chan has some other great tips on making yourself approachable.

So you go to a party and you see someone of great interest (SGI) across the room... There is nothing wrong with strategically positioning yourself in such a way as to increase your likelihood of meeting and striking up a conversation with this person.

Often times we girls move about in packs. Yes, going to the bathroom is a social activity for us. However, being perpetually imbedded in a herd of your nine closest girlfriends is not very conducive to being approached by a SGI... let alone any person with an XY chromosome.

For a guy, it is indeed very intimidating to approach a girl, let alone ten of them at once. And if he has an eye on a particular one, he hopes to God that she will need to go to the bathroom sometime during the course of the evening... (Oh wait, she'd probably bring her posse with her.)

Therefore, girls, try your best not to congeal en masse at social gatherings if you hope to meet a SGI. I know meeting new people is a very scary thing and you naturally cling to your girlfriends for support (and protection). But hiding inside a big group of girlfriends is not very conducive to getting a date... let alone one worth keeping.

So try to seek opportune times during the evening to casually saunter over to the drink table...ALONE. And when you excuse yourself to go to the restroom, try not to drag all your girlfriends along for the experience.

If you feel weird being by yourself and you must adhere to a mass of girls, at least be on the outskirts of the group. If possible, posture yourself in a way such that you would at least maintain a vestige of approachability by someone of the opposite sex.

Also, if you have a habit of talking exclusively to people you already know at social gatherings, this may very well be one way that you are "hiding from love"? Conversing with someone you already know feels safe? However, as I've said many times before, all good things in life require an element of risk. I'm not saying never talk to anyone you know at parties; just don't do this to the exclusion of meeting anyone else.

Another strategy inspired by a friend, is if you see a SGI across the room talking to someone else you know, go up to your friend to say hi. Social etiquette dictates that he or she would introduce you to the SGI, and voila--you are in. You now have a golden opportunity to start a conversation with the SGI.

Peanut Butter & Jelly

6) Clearly Communicating

After meeting Catherine, I told her that I wouldn't mind getting to know her better so she invited me to come and hang out with her and her friends in Las Vegas. I was really stoked. A few days later, when I called, by the sound of her voice something was not right. Catherine said, "You know, I don't think I'm that interested after all."

Obviously, I was both confused and disappointed. Why didn't she just say how she felt in the first place? Not only that, but I had already made travel plans and scheduled activities with friends in Las Vegas, which I wouldn't have if she was clear from the beginning she was not interested.

*"Sugar and spice,
And all things nice,
That's what little girls are made of."*[33]

Some girls are just too sweet and nice to let guys know how they feel. This is not cool. If a guy is making the moves, but you don't feel the same way, clearly send him some signals that you either want him to slow down or stop.

Be clear about how you feel about a guy. If a guy expresses interest in you, but you don't feel the same, don't give him the impression you do. Don't lead him on. If you're not sure how you feel, just say, "Thanks for asking. Can I get back to you in a few days?" If you only see him as a friend, just say, "I think it's best if we're just friends."

If you feel that a guy may be romantically interested in you, but you're not interested, then dis-connect yourself from him. This may include not going to functions he invited you to, being slow to respond to his e-mails or calls, becoming less engaging in conversation and so on.

If he is super dense and doesn't get your hints, you might want to tell one of his friends to knock some sense into his cranium. If even that fails, then the last resort would be to give him the silent treatment. If you do, be sure he is interested in you. Keep in mind that some guys are just charming and they're not necessarily interested in you. If you give the silent treatment and he's not interested in you, you may end up messing up the friendship.

This reminds me of Tanya. She thought I was interested in her and because she didn't feel the same way she gave me the silent treatment. This sucked for me because I was wondering what in the world was going on. We used to e-mail to say "hi" and stuff and then one day our communication stopped. At church, she looked away from me and avoided eye contact. Whenever we hung out with mutual friends, she wouldn't ask, "How are you, Mike?" or initiate any form of conversation.

Once she e-mailed a group of people to see if anyone was interested in attending the New Year Eve's event at Universal Studios City Walk, a cool hang-out spot in Hollywood, California. It just so happened that I, too, was thinking about going with some friends so I e-mailed her suggesting we all grab dinner together beforehand. She agreed.

---

33   Writer Unknown.

But when the event came, Tanya never called me when she got to City Walk to tell me where she and her friends were going to be. Nor did she contact me with any concern like, "Mike, I didn't see you at City Walk, just wanted to make sure you were OK." Absolutely nothing. I was hurt because it's just common courtesy to follow up with the people you invite.

She later admitted she was avoiding me because she didn't want me to think she was interested. My friendship with Tanya has never been the same since and will probably never return to normal. Needless to say, I'm disappointed losing a friend to something easily avoidable. I wish she had been upfront talking to me about things, rather than being evasive, which made me feel miserable. I'm sure she didn't try to make me feel bad on purpose, but all this would have been avoided had she talked things out from the get-go.

7) Let's Just Be Friends

Kate Chan has some insightful thoughts on how a girl can let a guy down in a nice way. Take it away, Kate.

If you are not that interested in a guy, but you wouldn't say your interest level is nil, you can slow down the frequency of contact by accepting his dates, but extending the intervals between the dates. For example, "Maybe not next week, but how about two weeks from now?" Your response time in returning his calls, and the length of your conversations, will also give him a clue to how interested/not interested you are in him. However, if your interest level ever falls to the point of nil, I would say it is best to give him the LJBF (Let's-Just-Be-Friends) speech, in a kind and straightforward manner.

However, girls, suppose you find yourself in a position where you no longer (or never was) interested in a guy, but he continues to call you/ask you out on dates without actually ever saying anything explicit about his intentions. I know it feels really uncomfortable bringing anything up because (a) you hate confrontation and don't want to hurt his feelings, and (b) you don't want to come off as being presumptuous.

If you find yourself in such a predicament, you can first try the indirect method of dropping hints that you are not interested, such as saying, "Sorry, I'm busy that night," with no attempts to reschedule. If the guy is perceptive, he will pick up on your subtle cues, and both of you will be spared the uncomfortable exchange of a Let's-Just-Be-Friends (LJBF) talk. However, guys are sometimes dense so... unfortunately, at times, you may need to initiate the DTR yourself.

So here is one way you can broach the topic in a kind and straightforward manner, without coming off as too presumptuous:

"So... I notice we've been talking on the phone/hanging out more, and I just wanted to clarify that I'm only interested in being friends."

If the guy is mature and respectful, he will say something like, "Yeah, that's fine. Thanks for letting me know."

See? That wasn't so painful, was it?

It's totally prudent for you to say no to most guys. Some guys think every girl should go out, at least once, with any guy who asks her out just to give him a chance. I don't agree with this at all. Many guys are not worthy of consideration. If you're not interested, just say no. Don't lead the guy on. This doesn't mean you can't be friends. It just means he doesn't get a date with you.

You might not like the guy who asked you out, but at least, show courtesy and thank him. It takes guts to ask you out, you know? It could be something short like, "Eddie, thanks for asking me, but I'm afraid I'm not interested."

When a guy tries to get to know you better try not to brush him off harshly saying, "No way, Josè!"[34] Some guys are super fragile and sensitive and may get emotionally scarred. Regardless of what the guy is like, be gracious in your response.

Let's hear what Christie Chong has to say about boundaries, mixed messages, and indecisiveness with girls:

Girls, it's important to be clear about where your boundaries are. Don't flirt and lead guys on, and then complain they are being sketchy. That's not fair. Be clear about your sketch-tolerance level. If a guy is doing something that makes you uncomfortable, let him know in a gentle way (not in a way that will embarrass him, and especially not in public). You can say, "Hey, usually I'm cool with <blank> because I know you're friendly, but when you do <blank>, it makes me a little uncomfortable. Just wanted to let you know..." Be careful not to put him on the spot though.[35]

---

34   Especially if his name is not Josè.
35   www.xanga.com/whatwomenwant

8) Staying True

If a guy asks you out for a date and you tell him you'll get back to him, please have the courtesy to do so within 48 hours. Anything longer would not be cool. You'll be leaving the guy hangin'.

He may spend needless time in mental anguish thinking any of the following:

- "Is she mad at me?"
- "Did I say something wrong?"
- "Will she ever get back to me?"
- "Did her e-mail response get lost in cyberspace?"

Sometimes you may not want to respond and just let things die down on its own, but trust me, a guy will never forget you left him hangin' like that.

This reminds me of the time I asked Teresa out. She told me she'd get back to me, but never did. Week after week, I was wondering to myself, "Is she going to get back to me?" Finally, I gave up on hearing from her. Needless to say, it was mentally draining for me. I later found out she didn't know how to say no so she swept everything under the rug.

One reason you may not want to give any response is because you don't want to hurt this guy's feelings or you're afraid the relationship would be a little awkward if you tell him no, but you would be hurting him more by not giving him a response after you've promised to.

A guy can't think of anything more cruel you can do than to promise to get back to him, only to leave him hangin'. You may not feel comfortable responding, but the point is not your comfort. The point is doing the right thing. Any guy who asks you out is worthy of a response. You may also briefly explain how you came to your decision, but if you prefer not to, don't feel like you have to.

Remember the Golden Rule.

"So whatever you wish that others would do to you, do also to them..."[36]

If you were the guy, you wouldn't want that to happen to you, right? Then why would you want to do this to a guy? If you make a promise you must keep it.

---

36   Matthew 7:12

"… Don't say anything you don't mean."[37]

Respond in a reasonable amount of time, not six months later. Obviously, if there has been a ridiculous elapse of time, ask his forgiveness. If you don't respond he will lose respect for you.

When you do ask for forgiveness, be specific (i.e. "Sorry, Larry, for not responding to you a few weeks ago when you asked me out. Will you forgive me?"). If you are lucky, your humility may win you back some respect.

Free tip: Pay attention to how he treats you after you say no. Lesser guys may show their anger or jealousy, say negative things about you, or avoid seeing or talking to you altogether. If this is his response, then surely you've made the right choice. A guy who can't take no is not worthy to be your man.

9) Don't Tell the Whole World

When a guy asks you out, don't tell everybody you know about it and make it seem as if he just asked you to marry him. He simply wants to get to know you better. The last thing he needs to hear is for everything to come full circle. This is what I mean… After Johnny asks you out, you tell all your friends so they ask Johnny, "Hey, we heard you asked Mandy out?" Johnny will feel uneasy knowing that you told about half the world. In fact, if you do this he may never ask you out again.

---

37   Matthew 5:22

Another reason why you shouldn't tell everybody is if you decide not to date Johnny and all the girls know about this they may put him on the guys-to-avoid list. The guys on this list might not be desperate, but the point is that girls will perceive them this way. And girls don't like being thought of as last resort (i.e. "Johnny only asked me out because Pamela rejected him. I'm not going to be his back-up.). Just because you're not a guy's #1 pick, doesn't mean that he might not be God's choice for you.

Telling a few of your girl friends Johnny asked you out is a great idea, but please choose wisely. Not everybody on the planet needs to know. Ask your girl friends to keep things hush-hush. What's the point of telling your friends if they aren't going to counsel and pray for you?

10) Only Once

If you initially said no to a guy, but later on are interested in him, say something to indicate you've changed your mind like, "Billy, about that picnic you suggested… I'd like to do that if you're still up for it." Keep in mind that some guys quickly move on so if you're not sure if he has, ask a few of his close friends what they think of your plan.

After a guy asks you out on a date, the ball is now in your court.[38] Even if you say no, the ball is still in your court because he can't do much to get to know you if you've given him the red light. If you want to show him the green light after you've already given him the red one, do something to indicate you are interested. Otherwise, he may still think you are giving him the red light.

Godly guys are a rare find. They're on the endangered species list just like pandas.[39] Unless God is giving you the red light when a godly guy asks you out, consider it. Some opportunities come only once.

Good luck, girls.

---

      38   This is a tennis term, which means that it's your move.
      39   There are only 1,590 pandas in the world, far greater than the number of godly single guys.

Book 3
How to Find True Love

Mike Toy & Audrey Jung

1) A Day to Remember

The Tune: Canon in D by Beethoven.
Pink flowers adorn the entire church.
Candles light the ceremony.
Music is in the air.
Love also is in the air.

Women in beautiful dresses.
Men in dark suits.
Boys playing the latest portable video games.
Girls chit-chatting away.
The back door swings wide open.
The wedding party walks down the aisle, starting with…

The ring bearer, a short five-year old boy, in a little man's suit.
Cute flower girls with dozens of pink long-stem roses.
Groomsmen with their bridesmaids.
Parents of the bride and groom.
Everyone is smiling.

Peanut Butter & Jelly

Then silence.
The tune changes to the Bridal Chorus by Wagner.
The moment we've all been waiting for…

Out comes the bride.
Brilliant white is her wedding gown.
Her dress drags behind her as she meanders ahead.
Ravishing and radiant, without blemish.

All stand.
Lights like paparazzi flash from cameras.
Arm in arm her father walks her to the front to meet her groom-to-be.
With watery eyes, her father hands her off to her man and says, "Take care of my girl."
After some general instructions, the minister asks them to repeat the vows.

The Groom and Bride Say:

I, _____, take you, _____, to be my wedded wife/husband.
To have and to hold, from this day forward,
for better, for worse, for richer, for poorer,
in sickness or in health, to love and to cherish
'till death do us part.

The minister says a few words of wisdom.
He ends with "You may now kiss the bride."
"Ladies and gentlemen, I present to you… Mr. and Mrs. _____"

The audience bursts out with claps and cheers.
The newlyweds exit the church and enter a stretch limo.
The sign on the back of the limo reads "Just Married!"
And away they go.

If you've been to American-style weddings, this will be far too familiar to you. Everything seems so picture perfect as if hardship will never come and the blues will never be sung. But do you ever wonder if life would be this blissful every day? Will they live with each other as one or will they bicker and fight over every small thing? Did they marry the right person? Are they compatible? Why did they get married?

These are among some of the most important questions you'll need to think through. A good choice in marriage will add sunshine and warmth to your life, but a bad choice will limit or even ruin you. It is better to be single than to be married to the wrong person. Few people prepare for or think about marriage like they should.

2) What is Marriage?

1) Marriage is temporary

"At the resurrection people will neither marry nor be given in marriage."[40]

In the long view, as awesome as marriage is, it is temporary. In heaven, people will not be married. I don't know how all this looks like. Perhaps this just goes to show that one ought to live for God alone. Your relationship with God is the only thing that will last through the ages.

2) Marriage is for companionship

"GOD said, 'It's not good for the Man to be alone; I'll make him a helper, a companion.'"[41]

When God created all the animals He created them both male and female, but with the human race Adam was it. Why didn't God create both male and female at the same time as opposed to creating Adam first? The Bible does not answer this question, but I suspect that perhaps in part, it was to underscore Adam's loneliness so when God finally brought Eve, he would realize what a good thing she was.

Imagine Adam naming all the animals "You're Mr. Hippo and you're Mrs. Hippo. You're Mr. Bunny and you're Mrs. Bunny. You're Mr. Rhino and you're Mrs. Rhino..." and after a while Adam may have realized how alone he was not having a companion like the rest of the animal kingdom.

When God finally presented Eve to Adam, Adam knew right away that life was much better with someone else. Who would argue there is a difference between watching the sunset with your special friend than your pet goldfish?

3) Marriage magnifies the glory and greatness of God

"Husbands, go all out in your love for your wives, exactly as Christ did for the church—a love marked by giving, not getting. Christ's love makes the church whole. His words evoke her beauty. Everything he does and says is designed to bring the best out of her, dressing her in dazzling white silk, radiant with holiness. And that is how husbands ought to love their wives... And this provides

---

[40] Matthew 22:30
[41] Genesis 2:18

a good picture of how each husband is to treat his wife, loving himself in loving her, and how each wife is to honor her husband."[42]

A person's marriage ought to reflect Christ's marriage to the church. A husband's love for his wife ought to mirror Christ's love to the degree he even lays down that which is most important to him, his very life. Wives are to submit to their husbands as to the Lord.[43] God is to be glorified in marriage.

3) Gotta-Have Qualities

1) You both must live a life of abandon to God

Life revolves around God and no other. In the course of life, consider yourself fortunate to know even a few who strive to honor God with their whole lives.

2) You both must love God's Truth

You must have a passion to glorify God through obedient living to God's truth. No one is perfect in this, but are you making a valiant effort to live out God's ways?

3) You both must love people

Do you have a heart for people? Do you talk about how to serve so-and-so? Are you sensitive to the needs of people? Do you connect with those who don't know Jesus? Do you encourage believers to faithfulness and good works? A person in tune with God would also be in tune with what God cares about, namely people.

---

    42   Ephesians 5:25-30

    43   Ephesians 5:22 says, "Wives, understand and support your husband in ways that show your support for Christ." The terms *submit* and *submission* may carry a negative connotation to some, but this is not how I'm using it. God considers the husband the final decision-maker in the home. As long as the situation is non-moral, a wife is to follow her husband's lead. With that said, a husband would be a fool not to seriously consider the thoughts and opinions of his wife. Both husband and wife are equal in worth before God, but their roles differ.

4) You both must have chemistry

"Dating is a like a job interview. Not only do you need the right qualifications, but you also need the right chemistry."[44]

Ask yourself:

- "Do I trust this person?"
- "Is this person approachable?"
- "Are we socially compatible?"
- "Is this person fun to be with?"
- "Do I enjoy being with this person?"
- "Do I feel comfortable sharing about myself with this person?"

4) Nice-to-Have Qualities

- Beauty: She has long hair and a nice complexion.
- Nationality: She is Chinese.
- Height: He is at least 4'10".
- Age: He is at least two years older than me.
- Dress: He dresses nicely, not like a slob.
- Entertainment: She enjoys dancing and going to see movies.

---

44 Gary Ho. A UC Berkeley student par excellence.

- Personality: She is energetic and fun to be with.
- Employment: He is a big executive in a Fortune 500 company.
- Wealth: He makes over $1,000,000 per year.
- Athleticism: She is a gold medal gymnast.
- Sociality: My friends enjoy his company.
- Power: He is persuasive.
- Cooking: She makes dim sum.[45]
- Handyman: He knows how to fix things around the house.
- Leisure: She likes traveling to different places.
- Music: She knows how to play the piano.
- Education: He has at least a high school degree.
- Time: He spends quality time with me every week.
- Cordiality: She respects me.
- Stewardship: She doesn't buy unnecessary items.
- Maintenance: She is easily pleased with simple things.
- Language: He speaks perfect Cantonese.
- Culture: He understands the Asian way of thinking.

Desiring any or all of these preferences in a potential spouse is perfectly fine. Just don't think you will find someone who has all your nice-to-have preferences.

5) 10 Things You Don't Wanna Do

1) Don't be jealous

Often times your emotions indicate your value system. If you feel possessive or jealous because the girl you like doesn't feel the same way about you, it tells you something about yourself. Examples of possessive and jealous thinking include:

- "I want her to like me and me only."
- "I don't want her to talk to anyone, but me."
- "I can't get her off my mind. I need her love."
- "I don't want her praising anyone except for me."

---

45   Cantonese appetizers.

You might not verbalize it, but that might be exactly what's going through your mind. Ask yourself, "Do I have the right to feel possessive about this person?" The answer is obviously no. You think winning her heart is the key to happiness, but she doesn't belong to you.

Simply put, you have no rights over anyone or anything. You are a servant of Jesus.

"... I have been crucified with Christ... The life you see me living is not 'mine,' but it is lived by faith in the Son of God, who loved me and gave himself for me."[46]

If you have been crucified with Christ, then you have no right to be possessive. Acknowledge your wrong way of thinking and ask God to renew your mind with the truth that you are here to serve Him, not to get your own way. If you don't, your sinful attitude will plunge you into further misery.

Be reminded of a few things:

- You are significant, not based on whether or not the person reciprocates, but simply because God declared you are.
- If you believe God provides for all your needs, you won't view the others as competition, but as people to love and serve.
- Trust that God is good. God wants to bless you with good things. If this person is part of God's plan for you, the both of you will be together despite all odds.

A simple prayer could be:

Lord,

Please forgive me for believing that my happiness depends on how this girl feels about me. Help me trust in you and your desires for my life.

Amen.

2) Don't date someone just because you like him or her

You notice how he or she looks, laughs, smiles, interacts, and your feelings grow for the person. You start thinking, "So-and-so is kinda cool. I wouldn't mind getting to know him or her better." Then you start to replay conversations you've had with him or her in slow motion. You start to miss

---

[46] Galatians 2:20

the person when he or she is not around. What's happening to you? In essence, you are falling in love.

Just because you fall in love doesn't mean you should date that person. Putting the other person's best interest before your own may mean just being friends and nothing more. This may involve denying your feelings for this person as hard as it may seem.

3) Don't date someone just because he or she likes you

It feels great to know someone is interested in you. In fact, you might start liking that person, too, and think, "Gosh, a person who is interested in me can't be too bad. Maybe we should get to know each other better." Soon enough, one thing leads to the next.

Getting attention from the opposite sex is nice, but that does not warrant dating him or her. Get over yourself. Resist the pleasure of knowing that someone likes you when it's a clear sign that it wouldn't be a good match.

4) Don't deceive yourself

Never underestimate the power of your emotions over sound judgment when you are in love. Feelings are tremendously deceptive.

"The heart is hopelessly dark and deceitful, a puzzle that no one can figure out." [47]

When you're in love, your feelings and emotions cloud your judgment and objectivity. You tend to think that the other person is an angel or a Godsend so you no longer evaluate the relationship with an open mind. Perhaps unconsciously, you choose not to see certain character flaws in the other person because you're hoping that love will blossom and things would work out.

Pay attention to how the person you're interested in carries himself or herself. For example, if the guy is always breaking his promises, is he a man of his word? If the girl is constantly thinking about herself, does she have a heart to serve others? If you are not seeing flaws in the other person you may be emotionally blind, seeing only what you want to see.

---

47   Jeremiah 17:9

5) Don't allow nice-to-haves become more important than your gotta-haves

Many guys say that godliness is a gotta-have in a potential spouse, but in reality they are looking for a pretty girl who just happens to be a professing Christian. If godliness in a girl doesn't at least attract you, perhaps you are not as godly as you think you are.

Girls need to be honest with themselves, too. Some girls say they want a guy who has a big heart for God, but what they may mean is that they're looking for a guy who has lots of money, can get her whatever she wants, and if he's a believer what could it hurt?

Don't allow nice-to-haves (i.e. a person's family background, education, or wealth) become so important that you overlook someone because of it. It is possible that the person whom God has in mind for you may not have many of the nice-to-have preferences you're looking for (i.e. You may realize you can live with someone who isn't a workout buff.).

The looser you hold these nice-to-have qualities, the better your chances will be. Some people have regrettably passed up potential spouses because they were missing a few nice-to-have qualities. Don't let it happen to you. It's hard enough finding someone with your must-have qualities. Don't unnecessarily narrow your pool of choices.

6) Don't neglect cultivating other friendships

When you're in love you'll want to spend all your time with your special friend, which may result in neglecting other friendships. You'll be passing up wonderful opportunities to know and serve others. The body of Christ needs people like you to shape and mold them and vice versa.

Miltinnie Yih[48] comments: "Dating should not be done in 'isolation', where you don't know the other person outside of just exclusively hanging out with him or her. It's good to see how the other person treats his or her other friends, family, etc. This way, there is some accountability in the relationship."

---

48   Miltinnie Yih has co-authored Celebrate the Seasons (NavPress) and was a contributing writer for the Women's Study Bible (Thomas Nelson)

7) Don't marry a project

Don't marry someone thinking you'll be able to help him or her overcome major problems (i.e. temper tantrums, communication issues, character flaws…). Many people think once they get married, they can change the other person. Not only is this almost never true, but marrying such a person can yield some disastrous results.

If you can't change a person before marriage, what makes you think something magical would happen once you say, "I do"? These two words do not change a person's character. His or her problems won't disappear all of a sudden.

People hardly change. The way people are today is how they will most likely be 10 years from now. Have you known a lazy person who became gung-ho? Have you known a hermit who became a social butterfly? Have you known a high-maintenance person who became low-maintenance?

The exceptions are so few that you're unlikely to beat the odds. What you see is what you get. If you don't like what you see, then exit.

8) Don't rush into marriage

Let's hear Derek's story:

"Jessica and I were a great match when we started dating. In fact, I thought she was the perfect one for me until eight months into the relationship. At that time I noticed she didn't seem to care about people as much as I initially thought. Though we talked about this, she didn't want to change. I'm glad I spent time getting to know her. If I didn't, we would have married and I wouldn't have ever felt we are on the same page loving and serving people around us."

Some people feel so in love that they rush into marriage thinking, "Why wait? Aren't we perfect for each other?" The downside of this is that they may not know each other all that well or have considered how things would work out. In many cases this spells disaster.

Early in the relationship, people don't want to show their true colors, but after several months they may let their guard down. When that happens, you can reevaluate your relationship. Don't rush into marriage. It is a permanent and binding vow.

9) Don't think God owes you a spouse

You get mad at God when you don't get what you want. You may complain you've done so much for God over so many years, but God has yet to provide you with a wonderful spouse. You start to think God gave you a raw deal.

This is a gross misunderstanding of what you truly deserve. You do not deserve a spouse, a house, savings, a car, or anything. Nor do you deserve a job, good health, friends, or family. The only thing you truly deserve is a one-way ticket straight to hell.

"Work hard for sin your whole life and your pension is death."[49]

People who have a deep walk with God understand this concept. That's why they are always so thankful to God no matter what happens in their lives whether good or bad because they know they deserve far, far worse.

Understanding what you truly deserve will revolutionize your life. You won't feel like God owes you anything and you'll start to have the right perspective on life. You'll start to thank God for everything—the air you breathe, the food, friends, opportunities to serve…

10) Don't be yourself

This tip is mostly for guys. A girl likes a guy who can just be himself. This assumes being you is a good thing. If this is not true, then don't be yourself. Yeah, you heard me. Don't be yourself. If you're boring, don't be yourself. If you're lame, don't be yourself. If you're a couch potato, don't be yourself. If I'm talking to you, you've got to change. That's the only way you'll have any hope. Be someone you're not and hopefully that will eventually be who you are.

6) Giving Love a Chance

Hollywood tells us that love is at first sight. If you've seen chick flicks, you've probably noticed "the moment". This is the time when strangers lock eyes, everything is in slow-mo, and that love spark is ignited. If only life was as simple as Hollywood…

In reality, when it comes to our love lives, both guys and girls are superficial. What do I mean? Well, often times we don't look for the things God looks for so we poorly choose who we are and aren't attracted to. American media and our sin have tag teamed to mess up our understanding of what real love

[49] Romans 6:23

Peanut Butter & Jelly

and an ideal relationship are. This has had devastating effects in how we view the opposite sex and who we consider potential spouses.

For example, for some guys, the most important factor in a potential spouse is good looks. This becomes problematic because most girls do not look like the girls on magazines or in movies. So guys will pass up girls who would have made great wives because they're hoping for trophy girlfriends. For a girl, a possible important factor in a potential spouse may be how much money the guy makes. If the guy doesn't meet her standards she might not consider him.

This has led to the culture we are now living in. Everyone is looking for greener grass. The first question you need to ask yourself when considering a potential spouse is "Is God leading in this?" If He is, then you need to follow it. Whether God is leading in this relationship ought to be a much higher priority than whether you have chemistry and all the other questions.

We shrink our pool when we eliminate people as potentials even before we run them by God. Our way of thinking leaves out many godly guys and girls who won't make headlines. It takes a mature person to see through all the hoop-la generated by popular guys and girls to see something in less limelight people.

The problem with quickly putting the opposite sex on the friends-only ladder is that you may be putting the person that God wants you to marry there. Keep in mind that who you think is an ideal spouse for you may not be. And who you don't think would be a good spouse may very well be.

If you've been brainwashed by the media and have left your sin appetite unchecked, then there's a good chance your standards are way off. That's why it's not wise to dismiss someone just because he or she does not have quality #53, #85, #134 on your list. Be open to whom God might be leading you to marry. The person God has in mind for you might completely surprise you.

Before I get shot for being anti-romantic, I want to say that attraction is a mystery. Why are the people you are attracted to, not attracted to you? Why are the people you're not attracted to, attracted to you? The media tells us that love is at first sight. In the real world, love might not be at first, second, or third sight. It might be at tenth sight or twentieth sight. Sometimes, it can take weeks of getting to know someone until there is that spark. If you don't give people a chance and get to know them, you may never develop that spark. And even if there is no spark, it doesn't mean that God is not leading in it.

Give love a chance. Let God bring you your spouse. He's the best matchmaker of all.

Book 4
Got Love?—Questions & Answers

1) Dating

- "Is it OK to date with no intention of marriage?"

When you hang out with the opposite sex or become boyfriend-girlfriend, you may easily become romantically and emotionally involved. If you're not open to marrying this person, why would you invest so much of your heart by hanging out with or dating him or her anyway? Sure, it may be fun for a season, but you're bound to get hurt.

People's hearts are fragile and precious, not something to play around with. I am not saying you shouldn't make friends with the opposite sex. Just don't cross the line between being just friends and possibly something more if you're not in it for the long haul. Each person will have to decide where that line is.

- "How do I know if I'm ready to date or marry?"

Unless you are committed to God's will you are not ready. If you're not living a self-sacrificial life, you're not ready. If you're not passionate about serving those around you in Jesus' name, you're not ready. This is not a one-time thing, but rather a daily humble submission to God's will. Your life ought to reflect the highest regard to know God and to make Him known to others in your life. If God is not important to you now, He won't be when you're dating either.

Another important question to ask yourself is: Are you content in God?

"I know how to be brought low, and I know how to abound. In any and every circumstance, I have learned the secret of facing plenty and hunger, abundance and need."[50]

None of us will be perfectly content in God in this life. However, unless contentment characterizes both your life and the other person's, hold off on getting together. You will not be doing each other a favor.

Miltinnie Yih says, "It's essential that we are fairly secure in God before dating someone. Otherwise, we tend to rely on other people to affirm us for

---

50   Philippians 4:12

Peanut Butter & Jelly

our self-worth—especially in a dating relationship. We need to first make sure that we are right with God before entering a relationship that considers the potential of marriage."

- What are some great questions to ask on a first date?

Kate Chan has these great conversation starters for the first few dates. Check it out.

Some easy, first-date type of questions to start off with might be:

- *What are some things you enjoy doing in your free time?*
- *How did you decide to go into your career? Do you enjoy your career/job?*
- *Which college did you go to? What was your college experience like? What was your most memorable experience? If you could have done one thing differently, what would it be?*
- *What did you major in? Why did you choose that major?*
- *What extra-curricular activities were you involved in?*
- *Where did you grow up?*
- *What were you like in high school?*
- *How many siblings do you have? Are you close to them?*

- *Have you ever traveled to other countries? What was your favorite country or travel experience?*
- *Which church do you go to? How did you come to that church? How do you like it there?*
- *Are you involved in any small groups/ministry?*
- *What is your favorite book?*
- *What is your favorite movie?*
- *What kind of music do you like? Do you have a favorite band or artist?*
- *What is your favorite type of food?*
- *Are you more of a dog or cat person?*
- *Are you more of an introvert or extrovert?*
- *Are you the kind of person that sees the glass half-empty, or half-full?*
- *What are you passionate about? (See, this is less vague than, "What makes you happy?")*
- *Where do you see yourself in the next five years?*

Each of these questions can serve as a springboard for countless numbers of other potential conversation topics. Use your imagination and creativity.

Free tip: Ever heard of the saying, "A happy wife is a happy life"? Well, it's true when you hang out with a girl as well. If she's happy, you'll be happy, too. So keep her happy (i.e. buy her ice cream, tell her funny jokes, get her free chocolate samples from See's Candies…).

- "I'm afraid if I date so-and-so I might miss out on someone better (i.e. smarter, more beautiful, more charming…). Is that OK?"

Thanks for being honest. The truth of the matter is that you will always bump into people who are better than the person you date or marry. However, this attitude of "What's in it for me?" is not right.

The potential and beauty of a person is unleashed after marriage. How your spouse is going to turn out largely depends on how you are shaping him or her over the years. If you are not encouraging and building up your spouse toward Christ-likeness, don't be surprised if he or she turns out otherwise. And you won't be able to encourage the other person much if you aren't strongly grounded in God yourself.

If you've been faithfully cultivating a thankful heart to God, you will not think you are missing out on someone better because you'll be thankful to God for how He has blessed you. The absence of thankfulness leads to a whole host of problems.

- "I'm such a lonely heart. Many of my friends are married; some have kids, but just about all of them are at least dating. I don't like going by myself to weddings only to watch others relish the joy of marriage. Any thoughts?"

Perhaps the reason why you don't receive is because you don't ask. Keep praying for a godly spouse. Be persistent in asking. And if you've been asking, there's no guarantee you'll get what you want either. But what can you lose by asking? Keep in mind that godliness attracts godliness. If you want a godly spouse you need to be a godly person yourself. God will not waste a godly spouse on an ungodly person.

Meanwhile, surrender your desires saying,

Lord,

I desire to be married. Help me to be the person you want me to be. If it is not your will for me to be married, help me to be satisfied with your desires for my life. Give me strength to still praise and thank you.

Amen.

It is better to be single than to marry someone who does not cherish the things of God. Just because two Christians get married doesn't necessarily mean that God brought them together. People get married for wrong reasons all the time. Don't you be one of them.

We all want someone to watch the sunset with, someone to be there for us, someone who loves us unconditionally. However, sometimes what you think is best is not what God thinks is best for you. You may want that special friend, but God may think otherwise. Would you be OK with that?

- Guy: "I want a beautiful and fun-loving girl. Am I superficial?"

"Charm can mislead and beauty soon fades. The woman to be admired and praised is the woman who lives in the Fear-of-God."[51]

---

51   Proverbs 31:30

We are all naturally drawn to beauty and fun. The girl you're interested in must be attractive to you.[52] Why? Well, if you marry her you'll be looking at her the rest of your life. Sounds simple enough, huh? Be careful not to evaluate a girl simply on the outside though because looks can be deceptive and fleeting.

The general rule is that the better a catch a girl thinks she is, the less godly she is. Why? Well, such a girl expects people to revolve their lives around her; not hers around theirs. Consider yourself fortunate to find a girl who is godly for she is a rare and hard find. They're out there, but whether you cross paths with them in this lifetime is another story.

- Guy: "I'm interested in Annie. Should I let her know? If so, how?"

If she's a godly girl and you've prayed things through, it's not a bad idea to talk to her about your interest. It would suck to let go of this opportunity only to think back one day, "Gosh, Annie was an awesome girl. If only I took the effort to get to know her. Shucks."

It's better to ask and be turned down than to never have asked at all. Be courageous. Even if the girl tells you she's not interested in dating you, that's OK. Don't live with any regrets. Getting rejected may be painful for a few weeks (longer if you're the more sensitive type), but after that you'll be back on your feet again feeling like 1,000,000 bucks.

Loving people always involves risk. You can get hurt and disappointed. But if the girl is truly worth the risk, getting hurt is a small price to pay. Sure, it may permanently change the friendship, but it's better than not knowing what could have been.

- Guy: "I get really nervous on a date. I'm afraid if I don't impress my date, then she might not want to get to know me any further."

You shouldn't try to impress anyone. You live for an audience of one, namely, God. This does not mean that you should look like a slob and be yourself. What I mean is that you ought to focus your attention on getting to know the other person and seeing how you might spiritually encourage him or her.

---

52   Keep in mind that attraction alone will not sustain a relationship. There has to be more than just that (i.e. chemistry, conflict resolution skills, a heart for God...)

Peanut Butter & Jelly

Don't worry about the kind of car you drive or how romantic the date is. If that is all that impresses your date, you probably don't want to date such a superficial person anyway. In fact, why not try something simple? Just get some sandwiches and eat at the park. Afterward, toss a football or frisbee around or play a game of Horse (basketball). That way, you can get your exercise in, too.

- Girl: What should I do if I'm not sure where the guy is taking the friendship?

Allow the guy on his own initiative to express his feelings to you. If you haven't figured it out yet, guys like to be in the driver's seat. But obviously, if a guy doesn't DTR after five one-on-one dates, it'd be a good idea to encourage him to talk about things. Say something like, "Jason, I'm wondering where our friendship is going. Can we talk about it sometime?" If he sees the both of you just as friends then politely excuse yourself from hanging out with him so much.

- How do I know who God wants me to marry?

Sometimes, you don't know who God's choice is (unless, of course, the person's not a believer, then it's not God's will). This is just like the free will versus predestination debate. Does God have one person in mind for you? Or do you get to choose? The answer is both.

You can go through pre-marital counseling, ask your friends and family for their opinions, get to know your special friend for a long time and still not know for sure if this is the person you're supposed to be with the rest of your life.

That's where faith comes in. Do what you think God wants you to do. This is the element of risk you must take if you marry. Keep in mind that it is at least just as risky for your special friend to marry you. Risk cannot be eliminated, but it can be minimized.

2) Expectations

- Girl: "I'm really mad at my boyfriend because he forgot that today is our five-week anniversary. Hello? How can he? Doesn't he value our relationship?"

Sounds like you've got some unmet expectations and you can't have any expectation of anyone other than what he expressly agreed upon or is stated in the Bible (i.e. do not steal, do not lie, do not cheat…). For example, you cannot expect your boyfriend to invite you to go with his family to Hong Kong, nor say that you are the best girlfriend in the world, nor pick you up from the airport, nor take you to a nice restaurant. In fact you can't even expect him to remember your birthday.

Once you illegitimately expect something, you are bound to be disappointed. No person can perfectly satisfy you in every way you want. Disappointment leads to frustration. Frustration leads to anger. And when you are angry the last thing to enter your mind is how to love and serve him. So what should you do? Kill all your illegitimate expectations (i.e. "If he really loves me he would turn off the TV to go shopping with me.").

Even if you legitimately expect something, let's say your boyfriend agreed to pick you up from the airport at 10 a.m. and he doesn't get there until 1 p.m., don't hold this against him. Imagine blowing up at your boyfriend, "You were supposed to pick me up three hours ago. Where in the world were you?" How will that help the relationship?

Peanut Butter & Jelly

Instead be glad that he even showed up. Keep your expectations low. In fact, if you expect absolutely nothing of him, you'll be so thrilled by every nice thing he does for and says to you. It'll be beyond the call of duty. What a difference it would make if you responded to your boyfriend with, "Gosh! Am I glad to see you! I was getting worried something happened to you. Thank God you're OK."

Always give him the benefit of the doubt. Ask God to release you of anger and clothe you in His love. In general, guys are not as sharp and capable as girls. Guys easily forget things and have difficulty organizing their lives. For instance, most girls can multi-task with ease, but guys can only do one thing at a time. Doing even two or three things simultaneously will give any guy a headache. This conclusively proves that girls are superior to guys.[53]

Free Tip for Girls: Since God made you superior, please be understanding and patient with the guys in your life. They are just less evolved creatures. What can I say?

Free Tip for Girls: Do you want your man to love you more? If so, let him watch sports with his buddies, especially during the playoffs.

- Girl: I want to marry a guy who is going to be a missionary. What do you think about this?

Unless you feel God is calling you to have such a requirement, I wouldn't narrow my options so much. It shouldn't matter what vocation your potential husband is leaning toward. What if five years into the marriage, your husband feels God wants him to work in a vocation you didn't see coming? Don't marry a guy based on his vocation, but for who he is.

- Guy: If I don't get my girlfriend an engagement ring she wouldn't want to marry me. And it can't just be any ole ring either. It has to be from Tiffany's.[54]

If how you feel is correct, meaning your girlfriend is really like how you described, if I were you, I would probably not be with such a girl. This is a sign of a girl who is concerned about her standard of living. A godly girl

---

53   Guys, you should thank me for writing this. I've just lowered girls' expectations of you, which means you'll have fewer conflicts.

54   A jewelry store known for their little blue boxes. Many guys have traded fortunes to get a small piece of Tiffany's jewelry all in the name of love.

would not care about this. She knows that she is marrying a man, not a rock. Be careful of girls who are looking to you to fulfill their dreams.

- Guy: How much should I spend on an engagement ring?

Guess how much Billy Graham, the man whose live audience and radio broadcasts reached 2,000,000,000, spent on an engagement ring for Ruth Bell? Less than $165. I'm not speaking for you, but since I'm not half the man he is I shouldn't spend more than half of what he spent, namely, $82.50. Of course, that was in 1943 dollars, but still. He described the diamond on the ring as being "so big you could almost see it with a magnifying glass!"[55]

3) Conflicts

- How important is confliction resolution skills?

Very. Whenever two sinners come together you are bound to have conflicts. Perhaps it is related to how money should be used or saved, how time should be spent, how children should be raised, or anything else you can think of. Sometimes the conflict is petty. Other times, it requires a long conversation.

Before you marry, make observations about how you and your special friend deal with conflict. Do you sweep it under the rug? Do you insist on your way all the time? Do you try to see things from the other person's point of view?

The question is not whether or not you will have conflicts, but rather, are you willing to deal with them in a way that glorifies God? If you don't handle conflicts well as a single person, you sure are not going to manage them as a married couple. Prove yourself humble and look after the other person's interest.

- Why do so many Christian relationships fail?

That's cuz God is not in the picture. Just because the couple is Christian doesn't necessarily mean a thing. Most people get into romantic relationships with no intention of serving the other person's needs. They may think they do, but when the going gets tough, they bail.

People with the attitude of "What's in it for me?" are attracted by what the other person has to offer (e.g. "She's cute. If I can get her, then I'm going to

[55] Billy Graham, *Just As I Am*, P. 76.

be the man." or "He's got lots of money."). These people have no desire to love and serve others. It all comes down to how so-and-so can benefit me.

If you think you are a great catch (i.e. You think you're cute, smart, charming…), that's the best clue you really aren't. This is similar to calling yourself humble. The thought of it shows a lack of humility.

A person who thinks he or she is a great catch is obviously self-consumed. Such people rarely think about loving and serving other people because they are so absorbed with the three most important people in their lives, namely, me, myself, and I. They think the world revolves around them. They're looking to make sure no one else gets more attention than they do.

This attitude is the complete opposite of Christ's.

"If I, the Master and Teacher, washed your feet, you must now wash each other's feet. I've laid down a pattern for you. If you understand what I'm telling you, act like it—and live a blessed life."[56]

Usually, we only like certain people for what they can do for us. Jesus was different. He washed his disciples' feet, an extremely lowly task. Jesus served his friends. He truly loved them. Jesus even gave His life to ransom men. His attitude was to serve and love others without expectation of pay back. And we are to imitate His example. Without God changing someone's heart and mind, human relationships cannot be what they were designed to be.

4) Differences

- What if my girlfriend and I have different views on male and female roles?

If you can't agree on male and female roles, then you shouldn't get married. Why? Well, if you both have different understandings of authority and submission, unnecessary tension and quarreling will significantly hinder both your spiritual journeys.

Imagine a guy sharing with his wife, "I feel God wants us to go to China to serve people there. We should follow His lead" only to have her respond, "I don't need to follow you." This will devastate a marriage. If the person you're dating has a different view on roles, see if a relationship is even suitable.

Miltinnie Yih comments: "The most important thing here is the ability to come to agreement when there is a great difference in opinion. Who will

---

[56] John 13:12-17

be the tie-breaker? The woman needs to give that position of headship to her husband or they will be in for a constant battle. This doesn't mean that she has to be in submission completely to him—no wife is. It just means that she is committed to that as a goal in their marriage and will work on it. I also think that belief in the Bible as authoritative in one's life is extremely important."

5) Parents' Blessings

- Should I ask the girl's parents whether or not I could date her even if I don't know them?

I sure would. It doesn't hurt to let the girl's parents know you are interested in their daughter. This shows you respect and value them enough to ask for their blessings. This will be helpful especially if you end up marrying the girl. Her parents will be more apt to trust you because you were upfront with them and made them a part of the decision-making process. By knowing them, you can also learn a lot about the girl and the values she was brought up with.

- What do you have to say about in-laws?

Do you love your future parent in-laws as your own parents? Do you strive to build a quality relationship? Since you and your spouse are one, you ought to consider her family yours and care for them.

"Anyone who neglects to care for family members in need repudiates the faith. That's worse than refusing to believe in the first place."[57]

Relate to your potential future-in-laws as resources since they have many more years of life experience than you. Learn either what to do or what not to do. Keep them a vital part of your life.

- What if the parents are opposed to us dating or marrying each other?

I would never encourage a person to marry another if either sets of the parents are opposed for any reason no matter how ridiculous the reasons may be (i.e. "We don't like his career." "We don't like how short she is." "We don't think our grandchildren will look good if you marry him."). I can't give you a book, chapter, or verse to support this, but this is the ethos of the Bible. If God wants the couple to be married, He would change the parents' minds to give their blessings.

6) Counseling

- Should I get pre-marital counseling?

What could it hurt? In fact, why not get it before engagement? That way, it's easier to break things off if you might not be a good fit for each other. An experienced counselor may give you additional insights on areas you haven't thought about and pray for you. Marriage is a huge commitment. If I were you, I'd get as much help and prayer as I can. Don't overestimate your wisdom.

Miltinnie Yih comments: "Pre-marital counseling is like consulting—experience is worth a lot. Done with an experienced counselor, it is invaluable. Pre-marital counseling can help you both begin to deal with potential and actual problem areas and set up mechanisms to deal with them later."

---

57   1 Timothy 5:8

- How do I know if my girlfriend will be a submissive wife?

Check out how she relates to her parents, particularly her father. Does she respect him? Does she seek to please her father? Does she throw fits when her father asks her to do something or not do something? Does she make efforts to develop her relationship with her father? If she doesn't respect her father, the man she has known the longest, don't think she will beat the odds and respect you as her husband.

- How will I know if my boyfriend will be a spiritual leader?

The best thing to do is to get to know the people close to him. Does he take initiative with them? Does he lead spiritually? Does he serve and love others? Ask your father, brothers, and guy friends to check him out.

Guys can spot flaws and problems in other guys girls are oblivious to. I can't count how many times I've seen girls date or marry guys who make me scratch my head and ask, "What in the world does the girl see in this guy? He is such a loser. She's going to regret this."

- How long should a honeymoon be?

Take a life-long honeymoon. Seriously. A honeymoon is not just a weeklong thing in Kokomo[58] and then back to real life. Far be it. Enjoy and relish marriage. Don't take each other for granted. Ask God to help you cherish your spouse.

Aside from God, there should be no one more important to you. Some guys think having a wife takes away from ministry. No way. Loving and serving your wife is your ministry (at least a huge part of it). How can you be like Jesus to her if you aren't even around? How will you give an account to God one day when He asks you, "So why weren't you ever around to love your wife? I thought I told you 'to love your wife as Christ loved the church'?" I don't know about you, but the thought of giving an account to God sends chills up my spine.

Miltinnie Yih comments: "When God calls the two to become one, He means that they can synergistically work together in ministry and greatly <u>multiply their effectiveness and outreach.</u>[59] Married people need to pull

---

58   This exotic place is off the Florida Keys… at least that's what *The Beach Boys*, a popular band, say. Sounds like the place to be.

59   Ecclesiastes 4:9-12 says,

It's better to have a partner than go it alone.

Peanut Butter & Jelly

maintenance on their relationship regularly and devote the time and energy into growing the relationship come what may."

- What is a marriage check-up?

Many Christian marriages are loveless and joyless co-habitation arrangements with a roommate of the opposite sex. God forbid this to happen to you. Marriage ought to reflect the dynamic love relationship between Jesus and the church. Because we are all prone to laziness and spiritual lethargy it's helpful to do check-ups.

Check-ups are great opportunities to refocus on why you both are married, reaffirm your commitments, share your dreams and what you've been learning, serve one another and others, pray and read the Bible, and plan your future together.

How often should you do a marriage check-up? Some form of it should be done everyday. From time to time, it would be great just to have a date night or a weekend getaway. Don't just settle for a roommate of the opposite sex. Take advantage of your marriage to love and serve each other and glorify God.

Share the work, share the wealth.
And if one falls down, the other helps,
But if there's no one to help, tough!
Two in a bed warm each other.
Alone, you shiver all night.
By yourself you're unprotected.
With a friend you can face the worst.
Can you round up a third?
A three-stranded rope isn't easily snapped.

Book 5
Bonus Section: Extra! Extra! Read All About It!

Part 1—Just For Kicks

1) Social Etiquette for the Clueless

Tips on Honoring Girls

Note for guys: This point system helps you chart your progress. For example, opening a car door for a girl gets you two points. Carrying her shopping bags gets you three points and so on. At the end of the day count up your points to see how well you've done. Always try to beat your best score. Get it?

Opening Doors

1) Open the car door with one hand, motion with your other hand "After you," then gently shut the door after she gets into the car. Be careful not to shut the door too early, otherwise you may shut the door on her leg and that would not be a good thing. She may never let you open another door. In fact, she may never ride with you ever again. Girls have long memories of such things. **2 points for opening the door. 3 points for not injuring her in the process.**

2) After driving her back home, say, "I'll get the door." Then back up what you say with action otherwise you'll both be sitting in the car. **2 points.**

3) If she has stuff in your trunk, don't just pop the trunk for her. Take off your seatbelt, step out of the car, go to the trunk, open it, get her stuff, smile, and hand it to her saying, "Here you go." If she thanks you, respond with "Oh, it's my pleasure." **3 points.**

4) Open building doors for her. Make sure it is open the whole way, not just partially. When both of you are approaching a building door

make sure you are one step ahead so that you can open the door. If it is a heavy-looking door, go through the door first and hold it open so you won't strain your muscles. Motion with your other hand, "After you." **2 points per door.**

5) For revolving doors, allow her to go first. After doing so, go next and push the revolving door so both of you can get through. Make sure you don't let her do all the pushing. And don't get too excited about these doors, otherwise you may end up pushing way too hard and we all know what happens if you did that. **2 points.**

Car Maintenance

6) A girl cares about aesthetics and looks so before you pick her up, get a squeaky-clean car wash. If your car is dirty she may mention how filthy it is to her girl friends, which will not help your reputation. **5 points.**

7) If you anticipate driving her somewhere, use an air freshener[60] to neutralize the burgers and fries odor at least 24 hours beforehand. If your car has a strong fast food smell, use two. **1 point per air freshener.**

8) Before she goes on a road trip check her tire pressure. If they are a little flat, add air. Warning: Do not over inflate the tires. More does not necessarily mean better. **4 points.**

9) Check her windshield wiper fluid level. **2 points.**

10) Flip out her windshield wipers and clean off the dirt so she'll get a nice clean wipe every time. **2 points.**

11) Take it for an oil change if it is due. **2 points.**

12) See if it's time for a tire rotation. **2 points.**

13) Check the transmission fluid level when the engine is at normal operating temperature. **2 points.**

---

60   I highly recommend the Japanese brand *My Shaldan*, particularly the grapefruit one, which you can buy at Asian supermarkets for about $2.49. It will only last 2 weeks, but you'll love the smell of your car!

14) Make sure the power steering is working well. If you hear a squealing sound at the extremes, tighten the belt.[61] **4 points.**

15) Check the coolant level in the radiator. Just a side note: Coolant is a 50-50 mixture of anti-freeze, which is the street name, but it is actually ethylene-glycol, but let's not get too bogged down with the name, so just anti-freeze is good enough. Let's see, what did I want to say about it? Oh, yeah, I remember… coolant causes birth defects and other reproductive harm. Animals like drinking it because it is sweet, so make sure her kitty isn't around that stuff. If you need to add coolant, pour it in the right area. In other words, don't just pour it wherever you want. **3 points.**

16) Vacuum the interior of the car. **2 points.**

17) Clean the dash and steering wheel. **1 point.**

18) Make all the windows and mirrors spot free. **2 points.**

19) Oil the leather seats, only if it is leather, of course. If you can't tell whether the seat is leather or not, ask. Do not assume. **3 points.**

20) Wash her car and shine the wheels. **4 points.**

Driving

---

61   I'm not talking about the one around your waist.

21) When you are driving her around and get lost, take a deep breath, humble yourself, and ask the gas station dude for directions. She'll respect you for not being the typical guy who doesn't admit getting lost. Just don't overdo this and ask a gas station dude on every block, which may backfire and make her think you're really lost. **3 points for each of the first 3 gas station dudes you ask.**

22) If you are driving her around, get lost, run out of gas, don't have a GPS, nor cell phone reception, haven't seen civilization the last 100 miles, and only see cactuses and tumbleweed… pray for a miracle. **30 points if God delivers you.**

Walking

23) The most important thing in this section is not to step on her toes. If you do, that's bad. **2 points.**

24) Offer to walk her to her car or bus stop. If she asks, "Are you sure?" Reassure her you'll be happy to by saying, "Absolutely!" Usually, girls try to sound polite and nice by saying things like, "Are you sure?" It doesn't mean they don't want to take you up on your offer. **1 point for every block you walk.**

25) When walking with her on the sidewalk, walk on the side closest to the cars. This minimizes the chances of her being splashed by water puddles as cars race down the street. If you get splashed, make sure she notices what you did for her. You just became a barricade, man. If she does not notice, say something like, "Oh look, I got all wet." If she asks how you got wet say, "Well, in an effort to prevent cars from splashing puddles all over you I barricaded you at the cost of myself." If she asks, "Are you OK?" Respond with "I'm OK. Are you?" She'll say, "Yeah." End with, "Well, that's all that matters." **2 points for walking on the outside. 25 points if you get splashed by a puddle.**

26) When both of you are crossing the street, make sure you look both ways to see if a car is coming. Don't try to be slick and say, "When I give you the cue, let's race across the street. If you keep my pace, we'll avoid getting clobbered by the Mack truck. Ready… Set…" Use common sense. **2 points for looking both ways. 6 points for not being slick.**

27) If it is windy outside, walk in front of her to shield her from the wind. If she asks, "What are you doing?" Respond with, "I'm protecting you from the forces of nature." **3 points.**

28) When both of you come across a large puddle of water, take off your jacket and lay it over the puddle so she can step on it and cross the puddle. If the puddle is crazy huge, use your sweatshirt and dress shirt, too. What a gentleman! If you like your clothes too much to sacrifice them, carry her (i.e. piggy back) across. But don't do this if you have a weak back, otherwise you both might fall into the puddle. Still another suggestion is just to walk around the puddle. Actually, this might be easier. **2 points for walking around the puddle. 5 points for every layer of clothes you lay down. 15 points for carrying her across without falling. 5 points for carrying her across with falling.**

29) When you are ascending the stairs, allow her to go first so if she falls backwards you can catch her. When you are descending the stairs, go ahead of her so if she falls forward you can catch her. Hopefully, you can react quickly. If you are not sure of yourself, workout at the gym. **15 points if you catch her.**

Elevators

30) When the elevator comes, hold out your arm to prevent the elevator door from closing and with your free hand motion, "After you." Do the same thing when she arrives on her floor. **2 points.**

Food

> WOW! YOU SURE EAT FAST!

> THAT'S BECAUSE WHEN I EAT THAT'S ALL I DO. I KEEP CONVERSATION TO A MINIMUM TO FOCUS ON GETTING FOOD INTO MY STOMACH. SAY, IF YOU DON'T WANT YOUR BURGER, CAN I HELP YOU WITH IT?

31) When you are done chewing gum, don't just torpedo it out anywhere. Put it in a napkin before discarding. **1 point.**

32) After she is done eating at a restaurant, bus her tray. Do this only at a fast food place. **2 points.**

33) When you go out to eat, defer to her by asking, "Is there any place you have in mind?" If she does, go with her suggestion. Always put her preferences above your own. If she doesn't have a preference, read the following point. **2 points.**

34) When you go out for food sound decisive even if you don't care about where you eat. In other words, initiate. A girl likes it when the guy has a plan. She will most likely be fine with whatever you suggest. For example, ask, "Wanna go to Junior's Cheesecake?" Try to sound fun to be with. **2 points.**

35) At a nice restaurant, help her to her seat. Pull the chair out for her and push it in gently as she is sitting. **2 points.**

36) When you are fine dining and notice she is getting up from the table, stand up to acknowledge her. If she says, "Oh, you don't need to stand," reply with "It's my pleasure." **3 points.**

37) When you're eating, try having a conversation. I know it's hard, especially when you're in front of food, but if you don't, she may never eat with you again. Conversation shows you care more about her than eating your hamburger even though in actuality it may be a toss-up. Whatever you do, don't talk with your mouth full. God never intended for you to have both the wind and food pipes open together. **5 points for not talking with your mouth full. 3 points for every 15 minutes of meaningful conversation. 5 points if she doesn't have to administer the Heimlich Maneuver.**

38) When you're eating together, allow her to take the first bite before you devour your meal. Actually, don't devour it. Eat at her pace so you both finish eating at the same time. I know it's hard, but try. It's no fun for her to be with you if you gobble up all your food before she has had her third bite. **2 points.**

39) Before eating your food, offer some of your dish, "Would you like to try some of this?" This shows you are generous and enjoy sharing good things with her. **3 points.**

40) If she asks you, "Wow. Your shrimp taste great. May I have another?" do not bargain saying, "Only if I can have your lobster tail." Be generous. Give liberally without expecting anything in return. **4 points.**

41) When she offers you some of her dish, say "Sure." However, do not help yourself (i.e. stick your fork into her dish and grab all her steak flanks). Allow her to give some to you. Afterward, say, "Thanks," no matter how much or little she gives you. **2 points.**

42) After she's done eating, if she can't finish all her food do not say, "Can I finish your plate if you're not going to eat it?" Pretend she ate all her food. **3 points.**

43) When she has leftovers, ask a waiter or waitress for a take home box for her. Then box the food for her and hang on to it so she doesn't have to carry it around. **2 points for holding the box.**

44) When she needs a refill on soda or water, ask the waiter or waitress for her. **2 points.**

45) After eating the main course, ask her if she would like some dessert. You may even suggest something like, "I heard Serendipity's Frozen Hot Chocolate is real good." A girl loves dessert. Even if she is full, she still has room for it. **3 points.**

46) Do not burp before, during, or after a meal, especially those real long burps. You are not a one month old; you do not need to burp for your survival. **5 points.**

47) Pay for the girl. Sometimes she'll say, "Oh no, it's OK." Respond with "May I have the pleasure?" After that, she'll let you do so. **5 points for every $10 you spend.**

Caring

48) Offer to pray for things that matter to her (i.e. her project, her family troubles, direction for her life…). **2 points every time you pray.**

49) Follow up a few days later. For example, say something like, "How did your project go?" or "How's your family doing?" or "I want to share something with you…" **7 points.**

50) When shopping with her, carry her bags. **3 points for every shopping bag you carry.**

51) Be on time when meeting her, especially if it's the first time. Play a game in your own mind called, "I bet I can get there before she can." If you make a lunch plan be there 15 minutes early. If you have difficulty being on time, be there even earlier. **1 point for every minute you are early.**

52) If you are going to be late, call her and let her know. At the end of the call, sidestep your tardiness by saying, "Look forward to seeing you soon." **2 points.**

53) When she is late, don't say, "Gosh, you are 543 seconds late." Instead, greet her and smile as if she was on time. If she asked you how long you've been waiting, say, "Not long at all." **1 point for every minute you wait.**

54) When grocery shopping, make sure you push the shopping cart or carry the shopping basket. Don't try to make deals like, "If I push the shopping cart, can you bake me some cookies?" **1 point for every 5 minutes at the store.**

55) Help her put on and take off her coat when she enters or exits restaurants, museums, and other places. **2 points.**

56) When it rains pull up an umbrella over your heads. If the umbrella is too small to cover both your heads, make sure you, at least, cover her. Don't do this until you are outdoors. **1 point for every minute you hold the umbrella.**

57) If you don't have an umbrella, be creative and put together a makeshift one out of cardboard, newspaper, your jacket, or whatever. This is definitely going beyond the call of duty. **5 points for creativity. 15 points if your makeshift umbrella actually works.**

58) When she and her friends want a picture taken, volunteer to take it. Don't try to be in every picture. **1 point for every picture you take.**

59) When you give her a hug don't squeeze the life out of her. She needs oxygen. **3 points.**

60) Keep an extra jacket in the trunk of your car. Girls tend not to bring enough layers of clothes with them. Make sure it isn't the same jacket you haven't washed for two years and have used on numerous camping trips. **5 points if you have an extra jacket. 5 points if it is clean.**

61) Call the girl about 20 minutes after the time she should have gotten home just to make sure she got home OK. **5 points.**

62) Do not overdo things. For example, if you want to get to know a girl whom you recently met do not send five dozen long stem roses. This is too strong of a gesture. Do something that is appropriate based on the quality and depth of your friendship. **2 points.**

63) Do not buy her clothes as gifts. If the size is too small she may think she's overweight. If the size is too big she may think you think she's overweight. It's best to avoid it altogether. Never ask her what her weight is… unless you want to get slapped. **10 points.**

64) If she is carrying a bunch of stuff (i.e. books, laptop, Frappuccino…) carry it for her. **3 points.**

65) If the girl loses her wallet, look around for it. If you are in public, ask people if they saw the wallet. **1 point for every person you ask.**

66) If she sees a mouse, before she screams, jump between her and the mouse and say, "Do not fear. _____ (Insert your name) is here." **3 points for jumping. 5 points for not screaming first.**

67) If she is sick, make her some chicken soup and bring it to her. If you don't know how to make chicken soup, go to your grandma's house to get some of her home-cooked soup, pour it in a pot, and bring it to the sick one so it looks like you spent a lot of time and thought into making it. If she says, "Oh, you shouldn't have" respond with, "Don't mention it. I barely did anything." **3 points for every mile you travel to bring her soup.**

68) When she asks you for a favor, for example, "Are you free next Saturday? I need help moving some furniture," say, "I'd be happy to help out." **5 points for every 15 minutes of labor.**

69) If you are not available, say something like, "I'd love to, but I'm going to be out of town that day. Is there another day I can help?" If not, offer to find her a moving crew by saying something like, "My friends Arnold and Rocky can probably help. Lemme give them a call." **10 points for every able-bodied guy you can find.**

70) Make yourself approachable. Girls do not like asking favors they can do themselves, unless they are high maintenance. For example, if Jill tells you she is needs help moving a piano tell her, "If you need an extra hand I can help." **3 points.**

71) When you are using the bathroom at her home, make sure you put the toilet seat down before you leave. Countless girls have suggested this point to me. **3 points.**

72) Watch movies like *Sense and Sensibility*, *Pride and Prejudice*, and *Emma*. Learning 19th century chivalry makes you a huge hit here in the 21st century. **5 points for every movie.**

73) Take advantage of happenings in your neighborhood and community. Invite her to street fairs, hiking trips, musical performances, etc. **25 points for every event you organize.**

74) Buy all her and your friends copies of *Peanut Butter & Jelly*. That was a shameless plug. **5 points for every copy you give away.**

Airport

75) When dropping her off at the airport, don't just to drop her off and take off. Find parking so you can help her with her luggage. This does not mean you carry the smallest luggage and give her the big and heavy ones. Carry them all so all she needs to do is walk. **1 point for every 10 pounds of luggage you lug.**

76) As she enters the "Ticketed Passengers Only" zone, say something nice like "It was really good to see you. Let me know how things go." Wait, don't leave yet. Keep waving to her until she disappears. Don't wave in a way that makes it seem you are happy for her to leave, but in a way which shows you wish she didn't have to leave. It should be a little bit of a sad wave, but not too sad. If you still don't understand what I mean, call me. Whew. **5 points.**

77) When a girl says, "I'm coming to your city next week…" offer to pick her up from the airport. Sometimes a girl may throw subtle hints, which she secretly hopes you would pick up. What this girl is most likely saying is, "Can you pick me up from the airport?" **5 points for picking up the hint. 2 points for every mile you drive to pick her up from the airport and back.**

Birthdays

78) Remember special occasions like birthdays. **15 points for remembering her birthday.**

79) What I meant to convey in the previous point was not just to remember special occasions, but to do something for her which shows you remember (i.e. call her, send a birthday card, give a gift…). Don't just remember. Do something about it. Often times, girls say "It's the thought that counts." Don't buy this. This is girl-talk. They appreciate, not just the thought, but some form of action. **5 points for every $10 you spend.**

Conversation

80) The most important thing to know in this section is to assume you have bad breath even though you might not think so. Therefore, chew gum or pop a tic-tac in your mouth. Once the gum or tic-tac effect is gone, repeat the process. Otherwise, you might start to see birds dropping from the sky. **1 point for every piece of gum or tic-tac in your mouth.**

81) Try not to breathe into her face too much when you are talking, especially after eating onions or garlic. **3 points.**

82) Heard of the saying "Say it, Don't Spray It"? Make sure you don't splash people as you speak.[62] **3 points.**

83) When you get a cell phone call while talking to a girl, if appropriate, turn it to silent. Don't put her on hold. **2 points.**

84) Be creative in how you say things. For example, when a girl thanks you for something you did, instead of the ordinary "You're welcome" say, "The pleasure is mine." When a girl asks for a favor, instead of just saying the traditional "OK, I'll do it" say, "As you wish." The perfect words at the perfect time are a sure knockout. **2 points for every creative phrase you come up with.**

85) If you really enjoy her home-baked cookies, creatively praise and thank her. Say "Gosh, this is GREEEEEAAAAT. When you opened

---

62   Unless you are a killer whale at SeaWorld, splashing people is not cool.

up your cookie shop one day can I be your cookie monster?"[63] **2 points for being creative.**

86) When she is sharing something personal or important, affirm her by saying something like, "I hear ya," or "Wow, that must have been something," or "Thanks for sharing that." **1 point for every line of affirmation.**

87) To demonstrate your great listening skills, ask appropriate follow-up questions or summarize what she says by telling it back to her (i.e. "So it sounds like you had fun at the Great Wall of China, huh?"). **1 point each.**

88) Affirm a girl when she does something thoughtful. If she brings a card for everyone to sign, say something like, "Allison, that's really thoughtful of you." **2 points.**

89) Take the initiative to keep in touch with her. For example, if she plays violin in the symphony say, "Hey, let me know if you have rehearsal next week. I'd love to check it out." **3 points.**

90) Keep in touch by asking for help. For example, bring her some of your brownies and ask her to help you taste test them and suggest improvements. This way you'll have an excuse to see her. Think of excuses. **5 points.**

91) After talking on the phone, allow her to hang up first so she doesn't hear the click sound. **1 point.**

92) When you're visiting her home, notice the decorations and things hanging on the wall. Ask about them. Say something like, "Wow. Are these your graduation pictures?" "Who's this?" "How did you make that?" "What's the story behind this piece?" **3 points for every open-ended question.**

93) Be confident in what you say or do. For example, if you want to walk a girl home confidently say, "Walk you home?" as opposed to "You're a big girl. You don't need anyone to walk you home, right?" **2 points.**

---

63 A blue Sesame Street grouch who lives for cookies. What a great job!

Peanut Butter & Jelly

Writing

94) Handwrite a thank you card if she has done something for you. If you don't know how to pick out thank you cards, try a Snoopy[64] card. Girls all think he's cute. **5 points.**

95) Send her a postcard when you are out of town. **5 points.**

Dating Section

Stuff You Should Know

96) Dress up when you go out with her for special occasions. No t-shirts, jeans, or flip flops. Don't wear white socks with your dress shoes. Looks do matter. **8 points.**

97) If you have thinning hair, refrain from using gel because it further exposes your scalp by making your hair stick together. Mousse will be better. Then again, if she still likes you, you know she doesn't like you for your hair, which is freeing to know. **1 point.**

98) Don't forget to bring your wallet with you, especially if you are taking her out for a meal. **5 points.**

99) Don't just bring your wallet. You need to have a credit card or some cash in your wallet. Carry cash in proportion to her maintenance level. **5 points.**

100) If you have a car, pick the girl up from her home or wherever she is at. When you get to her home, don't honk. Park somewhere so you can get out of your car and ring the doorbell once. If she doesn't respond after 30 seconds, ring it again. If she still doesn't respond after 30 seconds, ring the door bell one more time. If she still-still doesn't respond, holler, in the most charming voice you can muster, "Sugar Pie. It's me. I'm here to pick up my Cinderella." If she still-still-still doesn't respond, maybe she isn't home after all. 2 points for not honking. 1 point for every time you have to ring the doorbell. 3 points if you holler.

101) When it rains pull an umbrella over her head, but not yours. If she is a sharp and observant girl, she'll say, "Oh no, you're all wet and cold." Respond with, "On the outside I'm actually freezing, but on

---

64   Charlie Brown's dog from Charles Schulz's Peanuts comic strip. He's mute. This means that he can't talk.

the inside I'm warm." She'll ask, "Huh? What do you mean you're warm on the inside?" Respond with, "Thoughts of you warm my heart." **10 points.**

102) Do not be a penny pitcher when you are with her. The saying "A penny saved is a penny earned" goes out the window. Spend those dollars. Don't be a cheapie. By the way, it's good for the economy. It's OK to toss a quarter into the wishing well. **1 point for every quarter you toss in.**

103) Do not be frugal and give her the chocolate Easter eggs you bought two or three years ago as a gift, especially when it's no where near Easter. **2 points for not doing this.**

104) The next time you ask the girl how she thinks the relationship is going she might list about 100 things she is dissatisfied with. After that, ask her, "Aside from these 100 things, I guess our relationship is going pretty good, huh?" **4 points.**

Fun Things

105) Take her to the jelly bean factory. At the end of the tour, prove your love by buying her a bag of jelly flops, which are less-than-perfect, priced-to-sell jelly beans. Reassure her they taste just as good as perfect ones and that they are no reflection of what you think of her. **3 points.**

106) If you are low on cash, pluck some flowers from an open field. **1 point per flower.**

107) The key to giving flowers is the presentation. Give her a Precious Moments[65] look and say, "Beautiful, I was walking through a field today, thought about you, and thought you might like these (Take the flowers out from behind you and give 'em to her). I got them just for you." **5 points.**

108) Every girl wants to be treated like a princess. Whatever you do, resist bargaining with her, "I'll treat you like a princess if you treat me like a king." **3 points.**

109) If you live near the ocean, make reservations at an ocean front restaurant. Get there before the sun sets so you can watch the sun go down. Free tip: To avoid permanent eye damage warn her not to look

---

65   Extremely lovable figurines known for their tear drop eyes.

Peanut Butter & Jelly

directly into the sun. **2 points for figuring out what time the sun sets. 3 points for warning her.**

110) When you are at a loss for ideas or things to do, ask a hotel concierge. They are familiar with special events and activities in town. **1 point.**

111) Surprise her. Show up at her workplace, school, or wherever she's at with a bouquet of flowers. Since all her co-workers, classmates, or friends will be there, it will be even more special. If they see the effort you put in they will constantly remind her over the next few days just how lucky she is to have a boyfriend like you. That way, she'll think about you everyday. Now isn't that worth it? **15 points.**

112) Surprise her. Get all your buddies to serenade her with you as the lead singer. Make sure every guy is dressed up, but not more than you. Quality is important. It's not just the thought that counts. If you and your group sound horrible, it's a big turn off. For beginners try *Earth Angel* by *The Penguins* or *My Girl* by *The Temptations*. It'd also be nice if you and your group are coordinated enough to sway from side to side on the right beats. Not necessary, but a plus. **50 points.**

113) If you're dancing and dip her, make sure you have enough strength to bring her back up. If you're not sure, don't do it. If you dip her and can't help her up or worse yet, drop her, that's bad. She may never dance with you again, let alone trust you. Don't say I didn't warn you. **2 points for each successful dip.**

114) When a girl is upset at something stupid you did or said, go find your Monopoly[66] game, dig out the "Get Out of Jail Free" card, give it to her and say, "I'd like to use this card now." **2 points.**

115) Let her win when you play board games. **3 points per game.**

116) Take her to a teddy bear making factory and make a teddy bear together. A normal teddy bear has only two eyes, not three. **10 points for making a 2-eyed teddy bear.**

117) Celebrate her 364 happy un-birthdays. Make her feel special everyday because she is. Think about it. Why would a nice girl in her right

---

66   This game is fun at the start, but friendships can be destroyed by the end of it.

mind go out with you? She's gotta be special. **1 point for each un-birthday celebration.**

Movies

118) When you are looking for seats in a movie theater, sit next to the stranger so she doesn't have to. If she doesn't like sitting next to the aisle you sit there instead. Put her teddy bear on the opposite side seat so she'll have a big teddy on one side and a little teddy on the other. If you still don't know who the big teddy is, you're pretty dense. **5 points for sitting next to a stranger. 10 points for using the teddy bear idea.**

119) When watching a movie at a theater, don't leave without her.

Here is a true story from my friend John Voelker:

"A former teaching teammate went to a movie with his date. After going to the restroom and deciding that he really didn't want to see that movie he left, totally forgetting that he had left his date in the movie theatre. No second dates for that dude. Where was his head anyway?"

Don't forget the girl, guys. Bad idea. She'll tell all her girl friends and none of them will ever go on a date with you either. **5 points.**

Eating

120) When you see an ice cream parlor say something like, "Hey, let's get some ice cream. My treat." Don't be boring and state things in the negative like, "You don't want any ice cream, right?" **3 points.**

121) Refrain from using discount coupons on your first date. This gives the impression you are cheap and don't value her even though you may. **3 points.**

122) Do not celebrate her birthday at McDonald's. **5 points.**

123) Well, if you must take her to McDonald's, do it right. Make sure both of you dress up. Lay out a tablecloth, set up silverware, china plates, and champagne glasses. You might even want to bring a small candle to light up for that special touch. If she asks you why you ordered the Happy Meal, tell her, "That's cuz you make me happy." **40 points.**

Peanut Butter & Jelly

124) If you don't like your Happy Meal toy, do not switch toys with her when she's not looking. **2 points.**

125) Do not take her on a free sample lunch date at Costco[67] unless you are buying her a $1.50 all-beef hot dog. It comes with soda and free refills. What a steal. **3 points.**

126) As much as you might want to go to a cheap all-you-can-eat Chinese buffet for your first date, resist it. Well, if you have to go, I'm not going to stop you. **5 points.**

127) Do not challenge her to a donut eating contest on your first date. Save this momentous event for a special occasion. But if you must, show her how many donuts you can eat. **1 point for each of the first 5 donuts you eat. 2 points for each additional donut you eat.**

128) When fine dining with her, do not ask the waitress, "So what items on this menu will give us the best bang for the buck?" **5 points for not asking this.**

129) When you invite a girl over for dinner, make sure you throw away all the food boxes, cans, and jars (i.e. Hamburger Helper, Campbell's Soup, Ragu, Pillsbury fudge mix) you used to make the meal. That way she'll give you even more credit because she'll think you made it from scratch. **7 points for every item you make.**

Amusement Parks

130) Take her to an amusement park where you can win her stuffed animals at carnival games. Try your luck playing basketball. You get three balls for $2. After you make two out of three baskets you get a small prize. After getting two small prizes, trade them in for a medium prize. After getting two medium prizes, trade them in for a big prize. After getting two big prizes, trade them in for a jumbo prize (i.e. a huge stuffed teddy bear made in China, filled with cheap styrofoam). By then you would have spent $40. Yeah, I know, I know. It's not worth it, but don't tell her that. Remember, you can't always be practical with girls. **1 point for every dollar you spend.**

---

67   A huge consumer food and products wholesale warehouse. They have an awesome return policy. I've returned things after five years and they gave me my money back. You might consider getting an engagement ring here. If one day, you and your wife run out of money, you can always return the ring for a refund.

131) If you don't want to spend $40 on a cheap styrofoam-filled teddy bear, play a grabbing machine, where you navigate a claw to drop over your desired object like a bear (not a real one, a stuffed one), grab it, lift it up, and bring it back to the opening where you can get it. Tip: You will have better luck if you grab the bear by the belly. **1 point for every dollar you spend.**

132) If you want to look like a real hero and win a big teddy bear for the girl and save some time while doing it, play the water shooting game where the goal is to shoot water from a pistol into a hole quick enough to be the first to pop the balloon. Pay off the other guys to play to lose so you emerge as the winner. Slick, huh? **1 point for every dollar you spend.**

133) If you suck at these games, go ahead and buy her a stuffed animal at the merchandise store when she goes to the restroom or something. After she emerges from the restroom, smile, look her in the eyes, and say, "Hunnie Bun, I think this bear has your name on it." Then take the bear from out behind you and hand it to her. **10 points.**

134) After you give her the bear, if she asks, "What do you mean 'It has my name on it?' I don't see my name on it," respond with "I wasn't speaking literally, Silly. I was speaking figuratively." When you sense misunderstanding you ought to clear the air as soon as possible. **5 points.**

135) Get the photographer to take your picture together so as you leave the amusement park that day, you can pick up a keyhole keychain. With this souvenir, you can see your photo through a small hole when you bring it into the light. **8 points.**

Snow/Ice Skating

136) Go on a snow trip. Build a snowman together. Don't just stand there and let her do all the work. **10 points.**

137) Whatever you do, resist the temptation of throwing a snowball at her, especially a densely packed one, which can injure her eye. **5 points.**

138) If she starts a snowball fight with you, throw a few snowballs back, but make sure you miss. The point of a snowball fight is not to win it, but to make yourself a moving target. You may even want to run

in the direction of the flight of some of her snowballs so you can get hit. That way she'll feel good about herself and think she has good aim. **1 point for every snowball you throw for a miss. 3 points for every snowball that hits you.**

139) Go ice-skating together. Try not to fall every 10 seconds. It's no fun for her to constantly pick you up. **1 point for every 15 minutes you don't fall.**

140) When falling on ice, don't drag her down with you. **3 points.**

141) If you don't know how to ice skate, don't pretend to be an Olympic championship skater. Spinning the poor girl around and throwing her in the air can land her in the hospital. **5 points.**

Hiking

142) If you're hiking in a national park and you see a 1,500 pound grizzly bear, run in the opposite direction as fast as you could. If you, at least, outrun her, you'll be OK. Just kidding. You're supposed to be her hero, Knucklehead. Don't just stand there. Do something. **10 points for doing something. 20 points if what you do saves both your lives. 50 points if what you do saves her life, but not yours.**

143) If you survive the grizzly bear attack, carve a heart with your names in it on a tree. **5 points.**

Complimenting

144) Sweet talk. This is a girl's love language. Cheesiness is OK. Here are a couple of examples:

- "Pumpkin, here's a box of California's finest sweets (Hand her a box of See's candies), but the world's finest sweet (Pause for two seconds for effect) is you."

- "Darling, I only think of you on two occasions (Pause for two seconds for effect): day and night."[68]

---

[68] Babyface has a song called *Two Occasions* that speaks of this.

- "Sweet Thing, I wouldn't trade you for all the gold at Fort Knox, but then again, it's not like I have access to the gold."

5 points for every cheesy line you come up with.

145) Take an astronomy class to learn about the star constellations in the heavens. The next time you look up at night say to the girl, "Look. It's the Big Dipper. Look over here. That's Orion. Look over there. That's Gemini." She'll remark, "Gosh, you sure know your stars." Respond with, "Thanks. But you know what the most beautiful star is?" She'll turn to you, waiting for your answer. Look into her eyes and say, "Her name is _____ (Say her name)." **20 points.**

146) If she looks nice, tell her, "Muffin, you look resplendent today… then again you're resplendent everyday." Make sure you say the latter phrase "then again…" otherwise she may ask, "Just today?" Then you'll be stuck. Actually, a come back line could be, "Oh no, of course not just today. You look resplendent everyday but on this day you're especially resplendent." Saved you there, didn't I? **3 points.**

147) At the end of your dates, say something nice to let her know how much you appreciate and value her, "_____ (Insert her name), thanks for talking with me. Actually, I did most of the talking. You were just listening to me ramble on and on. Gosh, I was afraid no girl would ever go out with me because they keep turning me down. They all thought I was a geek and socially awkward, but I'm glad you're not superficial like them. You looked beyond and saw something you like. That's why you're so cool." Just kidding. Don't say that. **5 points for not saying this.**

Holding Hands

148) When she goes to the women's room, instead of waiting around, go to the men's room to wash your hands so when you hold hands it'll be more sanitary. **1 point.**

149) When holding hands, try not to squeeze her hand too tightly. It may cut off circulation. **1 point.**

150) If she asks you why your palms are so sweaty tell her, "That's because I get real excited when I'm with you." **1 point.**

Peanut Butter & Jelly

151) If you tend to have sweaty palms dry your hands with some baby powder. If she likes babies, she'll associate you with them. You can only win. **1 point.**

152) If someone sees your chivalrous acts, he or she may comment, "Wow, you're such a gentleman." Respond with, "Actually, I'm not much of a gentleman. I just happen to be with a lady." Make sure you say this loud enough for everyone to hear. **2 points.**

Writing Love Letters, Etc.

153) Handwrite love letters. This personal touch will distinguish you. Here is a love letter Ronald Reagan, former American President, wrote to his wife Nancy when he was away from home.

The Sherry-Netherland

New York, N.Y.

Wed. July 15, 1953

Dear Nancy Pants

> *... I suppose some people would find it unusual that you and I can so easily span three thousand miles but in truth it comes very naturally. Man can't live without a heart and you are my heart, by far the nicest thing about me and so very necessary. There would be no life without you nor would I want any.*[69]

10 points for each masterfully-written letter.

154) Don't forget to write her name and address on the envelope before you drop it in the mailbox. "To: True Love" will not work. You may even want to write on the back of the envelope something like: "Mr. Postman, please handle with love and care. My love life is in your hands." Just kidding. Don't do that. Mr. Postman might get curious and open up your letter to read it.

155) Write her poems that rhyme. If you can't make it rhyme at least have a consistent number of syllables per line. If you can't even do that, well… I feel sorry for you. Just kidding. Give me a call. I may have poem templates to get you started. **5 points.**

---

69   *I Love You, Ronnie* written by Ronald Reagan

156) Write short notes or draw a silly picture with crayons depicting the two of you under a rainbow. The cheesier the better. **3 points.**

157) Go to an arts and craft store and be creative. Make her something nice. Personalize it with her name and an encouraging note. Make her a nice candle, scrapbook, ornament, picture frame, gift basket, pot, watercolor art, collage, and more. **10 points.**

158) When you give a gift make sure your gift is wrapped nicely. If you don't know how to gift wrap, have your sister or a female friend do it. For an extra nice touch, use a ribbon or a bow. The key is to make your gift look well thought out. **3 points.**

Meeting the Family

159) When you are meeting her parents for the first time, call them "Mr. and Mrs. So-and-So" unless they say something like, "Just call us Jim and Jane." **2 points.**

160) If her parents say to you, "Please make yourself at home," do not make yourself at home. Do not go through their cupboards. Do not go through their fridge. Do not help yourself to all the chocolate. Do not prop your feet on the coffee table. Be self-conscious. **1 point for refraining from each of these.**

161) If her parents say to you at the end of the night, "Thanks for coming by for dinner tonight. We should have you over again," do not say, "Sure, how about tomorrow night?" Instead, say something like, "Wow, does that mean you guys like me?" Just kidding. Say something like, "Well, that all depends on whether or not you're cooking my favorite dish." Just kidding again. Say something like, "Mr. and Mrs. So-and-So, I'd be honored to. I've heard so many wonderful things about you. I'm glad we finally met." **3 points.**

162) If she is coming over to your home to meet your family, clean up your bedroom, put all your dirty laundry in a basket, put all your comic books under your bed, spray air freshener everywhere, open windows for ventilation, take all your DVDs and video games off your bookcase, replace them with classics like *Romeo and Juliet*, *Pride & Prejudice*, and *The Rise and Fall of the Roman Empire*, replace your sports wall posters with Van Gogh prints, and clean the bathroom. **1 point for each action. 5 points for the bathroom.**

Peanut Butter & Jelly

163) If she is coming over to your home to meet your family and you have little siblings, pay them off. Tell them to only say good things about you and to not mention anything about you being a meanie, your bad habits, and how you copied homework off your middle school friends, etc. **3 points.**

Popping the Question

164) Convince her you are a great spiritual leader by encouraging her to read *Peanut Butter & Jelly*. Give her a closed book quiz after every chapter. If she is still dating you after all this, propose to her right away. She must be a great catch to put up with all this. **2 points for every quiz you give. 30 points for proposing.**

165) Don't say, "I love you." unless you can follow that up with "Will you marry me?" **3 points.**

166) To persuade a girl who is not sure how to respond to your wedding proposal look into her eyes and say, "You're not going to find anyone better. I'm as good as they come." **1 point.**

Pledge

Now that you know what to do, would you make this pledge and put things into action?

- I carefully read all points in *Social Etiquette for the Clueless*.
- I pledge to be the most honorable person I can be.

_____

Printed Name

_____

Signed Name

_____

Today's Date

2) How to Tell if a Guy Likes You

HOW DO I KNOW IF HE LIKES ME?

IF HE DOES, HE'LL ASK YOU IF YOU CAN MAKE FOOD.

THERE YOU ARE! SAY, CAN YOU COOK CUZ I'M STARVIN' LIKE MARVIN.

1) He says, "I like you."

2) He invites you to play video games with him and his geeky friends. You happen to be the only girl invited.

3) He stutters when he talks to you. He either really likes you or needs speech therapy.

4) When you even make eye contact, he turns bright red. He either really likes you or you constantly remind him of something embarrassing.

5) After a meal together, he offers to let you pay for him.

6) He asks you out to movies because no one else would go with him.

7) Sometimes his version of going out to movies is inviting himself to your home to watch your latest DVDs.

8) He's always asking you to let him borrow some money.

Peanut Butter & Jelly

9) When you remind him he borrowed money from you, he thinks you're kidding.

10) He asks you for your address because he wants to get multiple rebate checks, but is only allowed "one per household".

11) He's wondering if you can help him pick up something from the grocery store, even though he lives next to one.

12) When he comes over to your home, before you can welcome him in, he's already in and looking through all your cupboards and refrigerator for food.

13) When you say, "Make yourself at home," he takes it literally.

14) He sticks his hand into your cereal boxes for freebies and asks, "You don't want this, right?"

15) When you eat at In-N-Out, he offers to help you finish your fries and burger before you've had your second bite.

16) If he even bothers to ask you if it's OK for him to eat your food, he phrases it in a way that makes it hard for you to say no (i.e. "It's alright if I eat your shrimp, right?").

17) When you ask him to come over to help troubleshoot your computer he agrees to do so, but happens to be only free during your dinner time.

18) He brings you his dress shirts and wonders if you can iron them.

19) After your birthday has come and gone for weeks, he wishes you a "Happy Birthday" and adds, "It's the thought that counts, right?"

20) He writes you a Valentine's card, which starts off, "Dear Casandra" and "Casandra" is not your name.

21) When he brings you flowers, you wonder if he picked them from your neighbor's garden.

22) When he brings you flowers, he is fully prepared to defend the flowerness of dandelions.

23) If he ever buys you flowers for Valentine's Day, he buys them two whole weeks early when they are still reasonably priced… with the money you let him borrow.

24) When he takes you to a restaurant, he does just that. You're hoping one day he'd take you inside.

25) When he finally takes you inside a restaurant he allows you to pay your share first, then he not-so-discreetly slips in a "Buy One Meal, Get One Free" coupon.

26) He is into "killing many birds with one stone". When he takes you out for a meal, he says, "I'm taking you out today to celebrate your birthday, Valentine's, and Christmas. Did I forget anything?" You still end up paying for everything because he conveniently forgets his wallet.

27) When he brings you chocolate, he ends up helping himself to the whole box.

28) After he gives you a gift, he takes a Polaroid of you with the gift and says, "Don't you ever say I never gave you anything, OK? Here's the proof."

29) When he gives you a gift, he borrows it from you right away.

30) When he borrows the gift he gave you, you never see it again.

31) When he sees your parents he always tells them just how lucky they are to have a future son-in-law like him.

32) He always insists on role playing Star Wars lightsaber battles with you, but only if he gets to be the good guy and the good guy always wins.

3) Why Men Are Just Happier People[70]

1) What do you expect from such simple creatures?
2) Your last name stays put.
3) The garage is all yours.
4) Wedding plans take care of themselves.
5) Chocolate is just another snack.
6) You can be president.
7) Car mechanics tell you the truth.
8) You never have to drive to another gas station because this one's just too icky.
9) Same work, more pay.
10) Wrinkles add character.
11) Wedding dress—$5000; tux rental—$100.
12) The occasional well-rendered belch is practically expected.
13) New shoes don't cut, blister, or mangle your feet.
14) One mood, ALL the time.
15) Phone conversations are over in 30 seconds flat.
16) You know stuff about tanks.
17) A five-day vacation requires only one suitcase.
18) You can open all your own jars.
19) You get extra credit for the slightest act of thoughtfulness.

---

70   Writer Unknown

20) If someone forgets to invite you, he or she can still be your friend.

21) Everything on your face stays its original color.

22) Three pairs of shoes are more than enough.

23) You don't have to stop and think of which way to turn a nut on a bolt.

24) You are unable to see wrinkles in your clothes.

25) The same hairstyle lasts for years, maybe decades.

26) One wallet and one pair of shoes, one color, all seasons.

27) You can "do" your nails with a pocketknife.

28) You can do Christmas shopping for 25 relatives, on December 24, in 45 minutes.

4) The Secrets of Women's Language[71]

Keywords and Their Meanings (A Must-Read for Any Guy)

Fine:

This is the word women use at the end of any argument they feel they are right about but need to shut you up. Never use "fine" to describe how a girl looks. This will cause you to have one of those arguments.

Five minutes:

This is half an hour. It is equivalent to the five minutes your football game is going to last before you take out the trash, so it's an even trade.

Nothing:

This means something and you should be on your toes. "Nothing" is usually used to describe the feeling a girl has of wanting to turn you inside out, upside down, and backwards. "Nothing" usually signifies an argument will last "Five Minutes" and end with the word "Fine."

Go Ahead (with raised eyebrows):

This is a dare. One that will result in a girl getting upset over "Nothing" and will end with the word "Fine".

---

71   Writer Unknown

Go Ahead (normal eyebrows):

This means, "I give up" or "do what you want because I don't care". You will get a raised eyebrow "Go ahead" in just a few minutes, followed by "Nothing" and "Fine" and she will talk to you in about "Five Minutes" when she cools off.

Loud Sigh:

This is not actually a word, but is still often a verbal statement misunderstood by guys. A "Loud Sigh" means she thinks you are an idiot at that moment and wonders why she is wasting her time standing here and arguing with you over "Nothing."

Soft Sigh:

Again, not a word, but a verbal statement. "Soft Sighs" are one of the few things some guys actually understand. She is content. Your best bet is to not to move or breathe and she will stay content.

Oh:

This word followed by any statement is trouble. Example; "Oh, let me get that". Or, "Oh, I talked to him about what you were doing last night." If she says "Oh" before a statement, RUN, do not walk, to the nearest exit. She will tell you she is "Fine" when she is done tossing your clothes out the window, but do not expect her to talk to you for at least two days. "Oh" as the lead to a sentence usually signifies you are caught in a lie. Do not try to lie more to get out of it, or you will get raised eyebrow, "Go ahead" followed by acts so unspeakable we can't bring ourselves to write about them.

That's Okay:

This is one of the most dangerous statements a girl can say to a guy. "That's okay," means she wants to think long and hard before paying you retributions for whatever it is you have done.

"That's okay" is often used with the word "Fine" and used in conjunction with a raised eyebrow "Go ahead." At some point in the near future when she has plotted and planned, you are going to be in some mighty big trouble.

5) Top 10 Worse Ways to Start A DTR[72]

> I KNOW WE JUST MET FIVE SECONDS AGO, BUT CAN I ASK... ARE WE FRIENDS OR MORE THAN JUST FRIENDS?

> UMMMM. I NEED TO WASH MY HAIR NOW.

10) My mom told to me to do this because she said otherwise I'd die alone, so I was wondering...

9) I found out I have six weeks to live so...

8) I was at the monkey cages at the zoo and all of a sudden I thought of you and...

7) Remember when we use to say if we were both 30 and still single we would marry each other? Guess what birthday I have coming up?

6) I've really gotten tired of people asking me if we were dating so...

5) Since I spent a lot of money on this dinner, I actually wanted to ask you something...

4) I know we've never met, but I've read all your Xanga entries and...

3) I was thinking about the girls I have the most fun with and Katrina popped into my mind, but she's taken so...

2) I actually like your sister more but she's out of my league, so...

1) I'm sorry, what's your name again? Right... as I was saying...

---

[72] www.xanga.com/DefineTheRelationship

6) Bubba's List

Qualities of an Ideal Wife

Benjamin Buford Blue (AKA "Bubba") wrote this list of gotta-have and nice-to-have qualities. Making a list helps you sort out what you are looking for so I'd encourage you to come up with one.

For example, if one of your gotta-haves is a girl who doesn't smoke pot, well, because it is on your list, you will more likely avoid getting into a relationship with such a girl. Your list may change from time to time, but at least it provides guidelines you can work with. Then ask trusted friends what they think of your list. Of course, you want to be reasonable as well (example of being unreasonable: "She must be a real princess.").

Gotta-Have Qualities

1) Loves God with all her heart, soul, mind, and strength.

2) Broken and humble before God.

3) She intentionally looks for opportunities to bless and serve people, especially those who cannot repay her

4) Physically fit—she exercises regularly and stays in shape, which is important because we may end up running from lions and tigers and bears.

5) Does not idolize getting an engagement ring. Idolizing a ring can lead someone down the same dark path as Smeagol.[73] Not good.

6) Not given to the Princess Syndrome: "It's all about me."

7) Wouldn't think her husband is a loser if he didn't have enough money to buy food.

8) Willing to go wherever God may be calling her family, even to Skull Island[74], where savages and giant insects proliferate.

9) Obeys and honors her parents.

---

[73] *The Lord of the Rings* character who became possessed by an evil ring.
[74] The island where King Kong, an overgrown gorilla, lives. He must have eaten a lot of bananas to get to where he's at.

Peanut Butter & Jelly

10) Not critical of her husband's mistakes (i.e. She doesn't lecture me for forgetting to put detergent in the washing machine before a wash).

11) Rebukes her husband with love and gentleness when he sins or does or says something stupid.

12) Speaks her mind and shares her ideas freely.

13) Doesn't nag or whine.

14) Smiles a lot.

15) Laughs at her husband's wise cracks and jokes even if they're not that funny. Her laughter sounds natural, not forced.

16) Personable and Engaging. Someone who loves the company of people. She's a great conversationalist and listener.

17) Loves God's Word. She applies what the Holy Ghost convicts her of. She strives to obey God's commands.

18) Allows her husband to spiritually lead the family.

19) Quick to forgive.

20) Makes the most of every opportunity share Jesus with others.

21) Not a gossiper. She holds her tongue when she should.

22) Gentle and Tender.

23) Honest.

24) A cherry disposition like Mary Poppins[75] (i.e. warm & friendly).

25) Wise. She knows how to react in any given situation in a godly fashion.

26) Not short-tempered, easily frustrated, or moody (i.e. she must have self-control).

27) Stands up for what is right (at the appropriate time).

28) Prays her heart out.

---

75   A Disney movie nanny who makes household chores fun and easy for children.

29) She, her husband, and children are likely to be martyred. She needs to be OK with this.

Nice-To-Have Qualities

Food

30) Culinary skills. It'd be cool if she's a culinary school grad. If not, she could learn from the Food Network. Food is important. It's a matter of survival. Life or death.

31) Bakes great tasting cookies, brownies, etc...

Arts

32) Flexible in artistic expression. It'd be a nice to have at least one room in the home dedicated to the *The Lord of the Rings* (LOTR) theme.

33) It'd be nice if she was a LOTR fan.

34) It would not be cool if she was more of a LOTR fan than I am. That would be scary.

35) Likes going to Broadway musicals.

36) Musically inclined. She plays the piano and sings well. Knowing how to play other instruments is cool, too. The more the merrier.

Sleep Habits

37) Doesn't mind if her husband snores (not to say I do).

38) Doesn't snore while she's sleeping.

39) Doesn't snore while she's awake.

40) Doesn't bring me camping. I prefer to sleep on my cozy bed over in a tent any day.

Addictions

41) Not addicted to fine dining.

42) Not a heavy drinker.

43) Not a smoker.

Peanut Butter & Jelly

44) Doesn't chew tobacco.

Personality

45) Simple. Enjoys free things like watching the sunset, walking around the lake, peering out the window to see a rainbow...

46) Spontaneous and ready to do things on a dime. If I got last second event tickets, would she be ready to go that same night?

47) Takes initiative in introducing herself to others or getting to know others.

Miscellaneous

48) Loves doing household chores, laundry, home improvement projects, operating power tools, fixing cars and computer problems, ironing, gardening, etc. She jumps with joy at every opportunity to do this.

49) Wouldn't mind being picked up late regularly. She understands when a guy says he'd pick her up at 5 o'clock what he really means is 5 'ish, which could be anytime from 5 to 7 o'clock or even later.

50) Enjoys reading and writing.

51) Critical Thinker. She doesn't think what she hears is true just because someone said so.

52) Left-handed. I like watching how southpaws write. When we hold hands we can hold each other's dominant hand. Plus, it doesn't hurt to have someone who thinks right. Get it?

53) Southern hospitality. She is warm to outsiders and makes people feel welcomed and loved.

54) Doesn't have a long string of past boyfriends.

55) Medically trained. When I'm sick she can take care of me.

56) Enjoys learning about military campaigns and war history.

57) Plays sports.

58) Throws a perfect spiral (I'm talking about football).

59) Drives well. Has a good sense of direction.

60) She has absolutely wonderful parents, siblings, relatives, and friends.

61) Great kisser.

62) Learns from her past mistakes so as not to repeat them.

63) Has either a British or Australian accent.

64) Uses the same cell phone carrier so we can have free mobile-to-mobile minutes.

7) Boys to Men Boot Camp

Location and Dates: To Be Announced

Sponsor: Peanut Butter & Jelly Associates

Problem: Guys these days don't really know what it means to be a real man.

Purpose: To make a man out of a boy in an intense seven-day bootcamp.

Things that will be covered:

- Movies for discussion: *Gladiator*, *Rambo*, and *Braveheart*
- Cooking session—This is a rite of passage into manhood. Bake a turkey the right way. If it's not moist, tender, and juicy, you're out.
- Cleaning and Interior Design session—Make a dirty, unkempt house look like something neighbors would talk about.
- Overcoming fear session—Kill a moose or buffalo with a homemade weapon of your choice. Extra points if you use just your bare hands. This is a dangerous session. Many of you may be badly hurt and some of you may even get sent straight to heaven.
- Adventure session—Survive a challenging obstacle course. This includes crossing a burning bridge, swimming through crocodile-infested waters, jumping over a 500 foot drop with spikes on the bottom, and that's just the beginning. Learn how and when to take risks and chances. A bad decision can be fatal.
- Triathlon session—1500 meter swim, 40 kilometer bike ride, and 10 kilometer run.
- Outdoor survival session—You are stranded in the wilderness. Do you have what it takes to survive? This includes how to starting fires without matches, trapping small animals, and identifying which berries are eatable and which are poisonous.
- Muscle-building session—Develop strength without using steroids.
- Emotional therapy session—*How to Overcome Boo-boos* is designed for those who have been hurt or wounded by women. Strict

confidentiality.

- Arts appreciation session—Appreciate various forms of art (i.e. music, poetry, paintings, broadway shows...).
- History appreciation session—Learn about human civilization, war, and different cultures.
- Good Samaritan session—Develop a heart for those who are downtrodden, discouraged, and forgotten by society.
- Etiquette session—Treat a girl like a lady.
- Small talk session—Carry great conversations and connect heart-to-heart with people.
- Social skills session—Make yourself approachable, fun, and an all-around winner.
- Attention Grabbing session—Smile and wink with confidence.
- Sense of humor session—Get people to laugh and feel good about themselves.
- Romance session—Become a modern day Casanova.
- Wild-at-Heart session—Have spark, energy, and fire in everything you do.
- Confidence building session—Speak and carry yourself with coolness and sureness.
- Smart-Guy session—Process ideas wisely. Be in control of challenging situations, and come up with decisions worthy of others following.
- Spontaneous thinking session—Think creatively, on-your-feet, and outside-of-the-square.
- Conflict resolution session—Deal with disagreements, arguments, and dissension.
- Persuasion session—Understand how people are wired and how to convince them to your way of thinking.
- One-Life-to-Live session—Live in light of an eternal perspective, have the end goal in mind, and not waste any of your life on triviality.
- Addiction-weening session—Stop time-consuming behaviors like video gaming, collecting billions of DVDs, watching endless TV sports...

- Diet session—Eat well and avoid turning into a couch potato.
- Grooming session—Take care of your body and skin.
- Fashion session—Wear the right things for the right occasions. Be in style and look great.
- Oration session—Deliver memorable toasts of honor and speeches.
- Discipline session—Pump yourself to do what is right and good even when you don't feel like it.
- Spiritual integrity session—Become a man of your word, someone people respect and trust. A man of the Bible and prayer.

Only those who successfully complete all sessions in the boot camp will receive recognition. We're not exactly sure what the recognition entails because no one has ever gotten this far. Needless to say, not all guys will make it through the week. In fact, most will either quit by choice or fatigue, be disqualified, or drop dead.

So far we've had 1,967 participants and counting. We're hoping someone will make it to the finish line. The farthest anyone has gone was this dude who made it past the third day. Unfortunately, almost doesn't count. He was swallowed by a whale during the swimming portion of the triathlon.

If you plan to give this bootcamp a try, make sure you buy premium life insurance beforehand so that your beneficiaries can collect. We're not looking for just any guys. We're looking for a few good men. Do you have what it takes?

8) When I Fall in Love

Check out these photos sent in by couples (Well, it's actually from the same couple) who purchased *Peanut Butter & Jelly*, read it, and found their match made in heaven. Don't they look happy? It can happen to you.

Vancouver, British Columbia

Spanish Banks

Peanut Butter & Jelly

New York City

Boston

A New England Winter

Los Angeles

> I'VE GOT AN IDEA! IF WE DRESS UP LIKE THE 7 DWARVES WE CAN SNEAK IN FOR FREE!

San Diego

> HERE KITTY, KITTY, KITTY! HERE BOY!

> I ENJOY PETTING ZOOS, BUT ARE YOU SURE WE'RE SUPPOSED TO BE IN HERE?

The World Famous Zoo

Peanut Butter & Jelly

San Francisco

Part 2—Insights

1) Before You Say "I Do"

Learning each other's values will test compatibility and identify areas of strength and weakness. This helps evaluate whether your special friend is a suitable match and what potential conflicts might be.

Here are some questions to sift through both individually and together. Keep an eye on your special friend's reactions in various situations. It's easier to give the right answer than to live it out. For the sake of simplicity, the questions are phrased with the pronoun "you," but you can substitute "you" for either "him" or "her" (i.e. How would you describe him or her?).

Free Tip: To get to know how someone you're interested in, use *Peanut Butter & Jelly* as a prop. Say, "Hey, I picked up this cool book. Why don't you read it so we can discuss it?"

Peanut Butter & Jelly

Personality

1) How would you describe yourself? Why?
2) What excites you? Why?
3) What angers you? Why?
4) What worries you? Why?
5) What makes you smile? Why?
6) What makes you laugh? Why?
7) If you were an animal, what would you be? Why?
8) Are you a *Lord of the Rings* (LOTR) fan? Why or why not?
9) What character in LOTR are you most similar to? Why?
10) If you were Frodo Baggins of LOTR, would you destroy the ring or keep it for yourself? Why?
11) What are your best jokes?
12) What are your favorite cartoons? Why?
13) What are your favorite movies? Why?
14) What is your idea of a good time?
15) If you could write a book, what would you write about? Why?
16) If you were on international TV and could tell the world anything, what would you say? Why?
17) If you were stranded on an island, how would you try to get help?
18) If your home was on fire, what would you try to rescue (aside from the obvious like your pet goldfish)? Why?
19) Would you rescue a baby trapped in a burning building? Why or why not?
20) What are pet peeves or bad habits you can't stand?
21) Describe your past roommate living situations. How did they work out?
22) Do you take risks? Why or why not?
23) What kind of risks do you take, if any?
24) Are you afraid of failure? Why or why not?
25) Does your fear of failure inhibit you from taking steps of faith? Why or why not?
26) Are you concerned about what others think about you? Why or why not? If so, how?
27) Do you listen to others? Why or why not?
28) If someone corrected you how would you respond? Would you be defensive? Why or why not?
29) Do you dominate conversations? Why or why not?
30) Are you approachable to others? Why or why not?

31) Do you feel comfortable sharing your heart with your special friend? Why or why not?
32) Are you competitive? Why or why not?
33) What are your strengths and weaknesses? Why?
34) How do you respond after losing a sports game? Do you blame people? Get angry? Why or why not?
35) How do you react when your favorite sports team (or favorite whatever) loses? Why?
36) How do you react if something doesn't go your way or as planned? Why?
37) How would you react if you are late to an appointment? Would you apologize or call that person to let him or her know you'll be running late? Why or why not?
38) How would you react if your special friend accidentally spilled coffee all over your new car's interior or new clothes? Would you say "My new car!" or "Are you OK?" What is your first reaction? Why?
39) Do you volunteer to do unglamorous things (i.e. wash dishes after a luncheon, put chairs away after a meeting, pick up trash from the beach...)? Why or why not?
40) Are you always vying for highly public roles and visibility? Why or why not?
41) Do you procrastinate? Why or why not?
42) If all your friends wanted to eat Korean BBQ, but you prefer Japanese sushi, would you say anything or go along with them? Why or why not?
43) Do you do things even though you don't want to just because you know it needs to be done (i.e. rake leaves, shovel snow off the sidewalk, tend the garden...)? Why or why not?
44) Do you take initiative with people (i.e. invite them to a picnic, organize a dinner, put together a camping trip...)? Why or why not?
45) How does it make you feel to know you are better than others (i.e. You're more committed to God than John, more well-liked than Kelly, more talented than Sally)?
46) If you let someone borrow an item of value and the person returns it with scratches and dents, how would you respond? Why?
47) How do you respond when someone cuts you off on the freeway? Why?
48) How do you respond when something unpleasant happens to you (i.e. dealing with unresolved personal conflict, getting slandered, someone sneezing on your cheeseburger...)? Does that mess up your whole day or are you able to let it go and move on? Why?

49) Would you feel like a loser if you drove a beat up 1970 Cadillac[76]? Why or why not?

Hobbies & Leisure

50) What are your hobbies or things you enjoy? Why?
51) What would you do if you had an entire day off? A week? A month? A year? Why?
52) What are hobbies or interests you just can't stand (i.e. collecting rocks, growing plants, stuffing and mounting moose heads...)?
53) Do you spend too much time on your hobbies and interests? Why or why not?
54) Will you put your spouse before your hobbies? Why or why not?
55) Are you willing to learn to appreciate your spouse's hobbies and interests (i.e. visiting art museums, duck hunting, shooting paintballs...)? Why or why not?
56) Describe an ideal vacation.

Dreams

57) What dreams did you have growing up? What about now?
58) What would you ask God for if He gave you three wishes? Why?
59) If you win $100,000,000 how would you use it? Why?
60) If you could retire right now, how would you spend the rest of your life? Why?
61) What do you daydream about? Why?

---

76   This is not exactly a classic.

Friendships/Relationships

62) Describe an ideal friend.
63) Who are your closest friends? Why?
64) What is your Myers-Briggs indicator?
65) Describe an ideal romantic relationship.
66) Do you get energized or depleted when you are with people? Why?
67) What is the purpose of friendship?
68) What kinds of people do you gravitate towards? Why?
69) What kinds of people do you stay away from? Why?
70) What kinds of people like you? Why?
71) What kinds of people don't like you? Why?
72) Do you keep in touch with people? Why or why not?
73) Do you make efforts to get to know people outside of your comfort zone? Why or why not? If so, what kind?
74) Do you like meeting new people? Why or why not?
75) What does how you relate with people tell you about how you value them?
76) What are the best pieces of advice or words of wisdom you have ever received?
77) What are the best pieces of advice or words of wisdom you have ever given?
78) Do you keep your word or promises? Why or why not?
79) How do you feel when someone doesn't keep his word? Why?
80) Do you make sacrifices in order to serve others? Why or why not? If so, how?

Peanut Butter & Jelly

81) If you are splitting dessert, do you give the big piece away? Why or why not?
82) Do you have friends who are socially and physically awkward? Why or why not?
83) Do you consider yourself reliable and dependable? Why or why not?
84) Do others consider you reliable and dependable? Why or why not?
85) Do you feel jealous of others? Why or why not? If so, what are you jealous about?
86) Are you emotionally co-dependent on anyone? Why or why not? If so, whom?
87) Do you plan activities alone or with others? Why?
88) Do you commit acts of chivalry (i.e. open doors for people, carry bags for others, help people move...)? Why or why not?
89) How do you respond when someone opens doors for you or helps you carry things? Are you gracious? Why or why not?
90) Do you serve people nobody else cares about or you don't feel like serving? Why or why not? If so, how?
91) How do you use charm or guilt trips to manipulate people to do what you want? Why?
92) How do you favor those who have lots of money, good looks, more to offer...? Why?
93) Do you spend time trying to figure out the spiritual, physical, emotional needs of others and trying to meet them? Why or why not? If so, how?
94) What do you do, if anything, when you can't meet others' needs?
95) What is your view of authority (i.e. police, supervisors, government...)?
96) Do you prioritize your special friend's needs above your own? Why or why not? If so, how?
97) You've reminded your special friend several times not to forget something, but he or she still forgets, how do you respond? Why?
98) When you serve others, do you hope you will be repaid? Is it OK to hope to be repaid? Why or why not?
99) What motivates you to serve others (i.e. "Since God has done so much for me the least I can do is repay Him.")?
100) Do you cheerfully or begrudgingly serve others? Why?
101) How would it make you feel if your special friend was demanding of your time? Why?
102) If God wanted you to remain single for life, how would you respond? Why?

Money/Work

103) What is your view on money (i.e. "It belongs to me. I can do whatever I want with it")?
104) How do you spend your money?
105) Are you an impulsive buyer? Why or why not?
106) What does the Bible says about money?
107) Do you save money? Why or why not?
108) Do you invest your money? Why or why not?
109) Do you guard your heart from the love of money? Why or why not? If so, how?
110) Are you willing to marry someone who loves God, but is not rich? Why or why not?
111) How would you feel if God called you to work at McDonald's flipping burgers? Why?
112) How do you view blue collar workers (i.e. garbage collectors, custodians, hotel maids…)? Why?
113) How do you size people up based on their vocation or how much they make? Why or why not?
114) How would you feel if God called you to work the graveyard shift seven days a week for life?
115) What is your view of work (i.e. "If I had a lot of money I wouldn't work" or "I love working")?
116) What is the purpose of work?
117) If you can choose any career, what would you choose and why?
118) What % do you tip at restaurants? Why?

Gifts

119) When someone gives you an expensive gift, do you appreciate it or feel guilty? Do you feel the money could have been better spent? Why or why not?
120) Would you buy an expensive gift for another person? Why or why not?
121) How do you feel about treating yourself to gifts (i.e. a new sports car or a new Coach purse)? Why?
122) Do you give gifts to people? Why or why not?
123) What is the most memorable gift you have ever received?
124) What is the most thoughtful gift you have ever given?
125) If your spouse appreciates gifts (i.e. neckties or flowers…) would you get them for him or her? Why or why not? How would you feel about doing this?

Peanut Butter & Jelly

126) If your spouse wants a puppy, but you don't like puppies, would you still get a puppy for him or her? Why or why not?

Academics

127) Do you read? Why or why not?
128) What do you enjoy reading? Why?
129) What are your favorite books? Why?
130) Is what you are reading conducive for spiritual growth? If so, how?
131) When you have questions about certain topics (i.e. "How do planes fly?" or "Why is the sky blue?" or "Why do girls like flowers so much?") do you make an effort to discover the answers? Why or why not?
132) Do you boast about the college or high school you went to? Do you wear your school sweatshirt to show off? Why or why not?
133) How would you feel about yourself if you went to an unknown school as opposed to a top-notched university? Why?
134) What is the purpose of education?
135) What's your learning style? Why?

Bible

136) What is the Bible?
137) What is your favorite part of the Bible? Why?
138) What parts of the Bible are you most comfortable with? Why?
139) How do you study the Bible?
140) What do you do when you don't understand something in the Bible? Why?
141) If someone asks you something about the Bible you don't know the answer to, do you try to answer the question anyway or admit you don't know the answer? Will you tell the person you will get back to him at a later time when you get the chance to look into the subject further? Why or why not?
142) Do you try to apply what you learn from God? Why or why not? If so, how?
143) If you have doubts about God and/or the Bible would you admit them? Why or why not?

Prayer

144) What is prayer?
145) What do you pray about? Why?

146) Describe your prayer life.
147) Are you ashamed of praying in public? Why or why not?
148) When you shop or walk around town, do you pray for people you encounter? Why or why not?
149) What do you think about a believer who doesn't pray before a meal?

Evangelism

150) What is your view of people?
151) What are man's biggest problems? What are the solutions?
152) Do you care about people's spiritual condition? Why or why not? If so, how do you show it?
153) What is the gospel?
154) What is evangelism?
155) How do you feel about evangelism? Why?
156) How do you relate to those who don't know Jesus? Why?
157) How many unbelievers would consider you his or her friend (i.e. invite you to parties, socials, events…)?
158) Are you actively trying to reach people with the gospel? Why or why not? If so, how?
159) Have you any success with evangelism? Why or why not?
160) How do you define success in evangelism?
161) What can you do to improve your effectiveness in reaching the lost?
162) Would you stand up for what you believe even if that means people would ostracize you? Why or why not?
163) Does everyone who claims to be a follower of Jesus go to heaven? Why or why not?
164) Are you ever ashamed of identifying yourself with Jesus before your unbelieving friends? Why or why not?
165) If your biology professor asked the entire class, "Can someone tell me the origins of life?" would you stand up and tell everyone the truth? Why or why not?
166) Would you share your faith with strangers? Why or why not?
167) How would you feel if an unbeliever attacks your faith and calls believers hypocrites? What would you do or say, if anything?
168) Are you ashamed of street preachers (who preach the truth)? Why or why not?
169) Do you actively seek opportunities to share the gospel with people or do you wait for people to ask you? Why?
170) How is a person saved?
171) How would you share the gospel with an unbelieving friend?

172) What is the purpose of missions?
173) How would you respond if God commanded you to go to Zimbabwe, Africa to preach the gospel right now?

Church

174) What is church?
175) What is the role of church leadership?
176) Do you believe everything your church leader tells you? Why?
177) What are the roles of apostles, evangelists, prophets, pastors and teachers in today's church (Ephesians 4:11)?
178) What are your spiritual gifts? Have you been using them? Why or why not?

Theology

179) What is the purpose of life?
180) What is worship?
181) What is the nature of man? A good being? An evil being? Sinful from birth? Corrupted by the world? Why?
182) How does God need you in order to accomplish His purposes?
183) Do you believe in eternal rewards? Why or why not?
184) Do you believe God will hold you accountable for how you live your life?
185) What is heaven and hell? Does your view affect how you live your life? Why or why not?
186) How is a person justified (i.e. faith or works)? What are the implications for your view?
187) How has God forgiven you?
188) Can you lose your salvation? Why or why not? What are the implications for your view?
189) Who is God?
190) What does it mean to have a God-centered worldview?

Sin

191) Can a believer who doesn't go to church live a life that's pleasing to God? Why or why not?
192) If you were convicted about sin, how would you respond? Would you repent? Why or why not?
193) How do see abortion? Why?

194) Do you think about the injustices around the world (i.e. innocent people being mercilessly killed in unstable countries…)? Why or why not? If so, how does it make you feel?
195) How will you make provisions to guard your heart from becoming attracted to the opposite sex after you are married?
196) What might compromise your commitment to love your spouse and family? Why?
197) Do you filter out the things coming into your mind (i.e. when watching TV, reading magazines, listening to conversations…) or are you passive?
198) Are you discerning about what you watch and read? Why or why not?
199) How do you keep God's Word in mind throughout the day?
200) What sins do you struggle with? Why?
201) What are you doing to fight sin?
202) Do you constantly self-evaluate to fight personal sin and determine which areas you need to work on? If so, how?
203) How would you respond if someone said you were prideful and your faith was weak? Why?
204) If how you feel about something was in direct conflict with a Biblical command, what would you do? Why?
205) If someone sins against you, would you hold a grudge against him? Would you forgive him? Why or why not?
206) What does forgiveness look like?
207) If you sinned against someone, would you seek forgiveness? Why or why not?

Conflicts

208) How do you see conflicts? Good? Bad? Why?
209) Do you usually deal with conflicts? Why or why not? If so, how?
210) How would you like your special friend to deal with conflicts?
211) If something about your special friend was bugging you, would you bring it up? Why or why not?
212) When you have a disagreement how do you resolve it? Why?
213) Do you try to understand other people's point of view? Why or why not?
214) What happens when you can't agree on non-moral issues? Why?
215) If your special friend sinned, would you confront him or her? Why or why not?
216) If you sinned would you want your special friend to confront you? Why or why not?

Marriage

217) What is the husband's role?
218) What is the wife's role?
219) What is the father's role?
220) What is the mother's role?
221) What does it mean to lead someone spiritually?
222) What does it mean to submit?
223) For girls: If your husband wants you to be a homemaker, how would you feel about that?
224) For guys: What, if anything, would you do if other people mocked your wife for being a homemaker when she could have had a good paying job?
225) For guys: After marriage, are you planning to be chivalrous to your wife, give her gifts, and take her out on dates? Why or why not?
226) If your views on male and female roles are different than the Bible's, would you amend your views? Why or why not?
227) Would you still be committed to your spouse if he or she became a paraplegic? Why or why not?
228) If your spouse wanted a remodeled kitchen, would you do it? Why or why not?
229) It's 3:00 a.m.; you're in bed and your spouse wants a glass of water, will you get it for him or her? Why or why not? What will your attitude be?
230) If you were both stranded on an island and had only enough food for one person and you can't share, would you want your spouse to have it? Why or why not?

Family/Children

231) Describe your relationship with each member of your family.
232) How were you raised as a child?
233) What were your favorite childhood toys? Why?
234) What were your favorite childhood memories? Why?
235) What were your most traumatic childhood memories? Why?
236) If you could be parented all over again, how would you have liked to have been parented? Why?
237) Would you raise your children the way you were raised? Why or why not?
238) How do you view children? Why?
239) How does God view children?

240) Would you want your special friend to be your children's father or mother? Why or why not?
241) How many children do you want, if any? Why?
242) What is the purpose of having children?
243) How should children be raised? Why?
244) Where would you want to raise children? Why?
245) Would you send your children to public, private, or home school? Why?
246) Would your children's career choice affect how you view yourself as a parent? Why or why not?
247) Would you try to live your childhood dreams and ambitions through your children? Why or why not?
248) What does the Bible say about raising children?
249) What is your view on spanking?
250) How would you train children to have a heart after God? Why?
251) How would you measure success or failure as a parent? Why?

Parents

252) How will you love and serve both your family and your spouse's when you don't feel like it?
253) Would you make the effort to get to know and serve your spouse's and family's spiritual, emotional, and physical needs to the best of your ability? If so, how?
254) Do you love your parents? Your special friend's parents? How do you show it? If you don't, why not?
255) What does the way you interact with your parents tell you about your view of them?
256) What does the way your parents interact with you tell you about their view of you?
257) What were your parents' strengths and weaknesses?
258) What does the Bible say about honoring parents?
259) Do you make efforts to honor both your parents and your special friend's? How?
260) Do you plan on taking care of your parents' and your spouse's parents' needs, especially when they may not be able to care for themselves in the future? How?

Life and Death

261) What are things you would die for?
262) If you can go back in time and do life over again, what would you do differently and why?
263) How will you leave a lasting legacy? How would you like to be remembered? Why?
264) If you only had one week to live, how would you live?
265) What is the purpose of life?
266) What is your view of death? Good thing? Bad thing? Why?
267) If someone were dying, what would you do or say to comfort him? Why?
268) Are you willing to risk your life or your spouse's to do what God wants? Why or why not?

Miscellaneous

269) How does it make you feel to know people died translating the Bible into English so you can benefit hundreds of years later?
270) How would you feel if God asked you to wear a t-shirt that said "I Love Jesus"? Would you be embarrassed? Proud? Why?
271) If you can go back in time and meet anyone you want, who would you meet and why?
272) Do people ask you for help and advice? Why or why not?
273) When you need help or advice, who do you turn to?
274) Someone tells you that he or she is lonely, what would you do or say?
275) How do you respond in times of trial? Why?
276) Who do you turn to for help? Why?
277) How do you determine the will of God for non-moral issues (i.e. "Gosh, should I become a firefighter or a children's book writer?")?
278) Why do you compare yourself with others? How does it make you feel? Why?

2) My Journey in Understanding Girls

> YOU'RE WINKING AT ME. DO YOU LIKE ME OR SOMETHING?

> ACTUALLY, IT'S CUZ WHEN YOU TALK YOU SPIT IN MY EYE.

Pre-Kindergarten

The first time I ever liked a girl was when I was four years old in pre-kindergarten. I think her name started with "M" just like mine. It might have been Michelle or Melissa, but I don't remember. What I do remember is that I must have agitated her because I always tried to sit next to her during circle time.[77]

I didn't know why I wanted to sit next to her. I mean, I wasn't trying to have a conversation or anything. There was another boy who also tried to sit next to her, but because I was mature beyond my years I didn't viewed him as competition. I just lied. I knew what competition was even at that age. Now I need to repent.

The girls in my class were nice. They didn't bother me and I didn't bother them. The difference between the boys and girls was the girls weren't as rough as the boys; they were also better behaved and cleaner.

I couldn't figure out why girls were so different than boys. I scratched my head thinking, "Why would anyone want to play with a Barbie doll?" I found it weird that girls talked to their dolls. It's not like Barbie is a real

---

[77] This was a time where everyone sat in a circle to sing songs. My favorite pre-school song was *My Name is Stegosaurus*. It's a song about a dinosaur in case you couldn't figure that out.

person. I remember pretend-cooking in a plastic kitchen with some girls. I was bored out of my socks. What is that? It's not like you are actually making real food you can eat.

I was at a lost why none of the girls liked having fun looking for snails in the garden, riding tricycles super fast in circles, or building railroad tracks for choo-choo trains. This was my introduction to the world of girls.

Elementary School

When I was in first grade, I had a friend named Annie. One day, she moved from San Francisco to New York City. Because our mothers knew each other, they thought it'd be a good idea for us to keep in touch via snail mail. Annie wrote the first letter. At first, it was nice to receive something in the mail just for me, but then I felt obligated to write something back, which I didn't feel like doing. My mom pressured me to so eventually I wrote a letter back, mirroring what she wrote to me. I told her about my favorite cartoons and drew pictures of them. This was my introduction to the art of writing.

I learned in second grade that girls had cooties and we, boys, were supposed to stay away from them. This did not make any sense to me because if anyone had cooties that would be the boys. We were the ones who didn't wash our hands after using the bathroom. We were the ones who would pick up food from the ground and eat it.[78] We were the ones who would wipe our runny noses with our little hands and then wipe it against somebody else's clothes. Nevertheless, I went along with the boys and decided girls had cooties.

I remember liking this nice, fourth grade girl named Sarah when I was in third grade. Though Sarah had an identical twin sister, I still liked Sarah more. In fact, I started going to church, at least a few times, just to see her.

Even though summer school ended at 3 p.m. each day, I insisted that my mom didn't pick me up until 4 p.m. Why? Well, I was hoping to hang out with Sarah. We would sit on a short wall and talk about things like what we did for fun, what we liked eating, and kid stuff. I even offered her a banana sometimes. She returned the favor by taking me to the cafeteria to get cookies.

---

[78] I didn't know about the three-second rule until third grade. I don't know who came up with this, but this made-up rule says that even though food has fallen on the ground or floor if you picked it up within three seconds, it's still safe to eat. The guys in my class took advantage of this rule often.

Peanut Butter & Jelly

Once I tried to impress her by carrying 20 cups of lemonade on a tray back to our classroom. I was doing quite well until I reached the classroom door where I tipped the whole tray over. I may not have impressed her, but at least made things memorable. Sarah didn't lecture me or anything. She just helped me clean up the spill. I really appreciated that.

During elementary school, I wished I had more TLC (tender loving care). In dodgeball, I threw the red, rubber ball as hard at the girls as I would at the boys. The girls were a little bit afraid of me because I was quite a good aim. And I don't mean to brag about this, but since I was much buffer than the other Chinese kids in my class I threw the hardest. I guess dodge ball didn't exactly make me a lady's man.

There is another thing I should confess. When I was in fifth grade, I hit my classmate Barbara closed fist in the stomach once. She started to cry. I felt kinda bad about it afterwards, but honestly, I didn't hit her at full strength. I held back. I also knew I was going to be in some mighty big trouble.

Before you consider me a meanie, you should know the whole story. You see, Barbara and I were playing handball in the school yard where I beat her fair and square. She was so upset she kicked the rubber ball against the wall and it bounced off and hit me on my Achilles' heel.[79] So that's why I punched her. I'm not excusing myself. I shouldn't have. If you're reading this, Barbara, will you forgive me?

Middle School

During this time the boys decided that girls' cooties weren't that bad after all. In fact, they can be girlfriends. I had no idea how boyfriend-girlfriend worked. All I knew was if a guy liked a girl and vice-versa they would "go out". Sometimes they would even hold hands. This was way beyond my level of comprehension. Why would you want to hold hands? How is it beneficial to hold hands?

The only guys who had girlfriends were the popular and fun ones so I was out. All my friends were guys. We played hours and hours of basketball together, which wasn't exactly the way into a girl's heart, but I didn't really care either.

I remember a real nice female classmate named Kellie. She regularly mentioned to me, "Mike, you're always wearing the same clothes day after day." I didn't know how to respond. I thought to myself, "Now,

---

[79] My weak spot if you know what I mean.

what's wrong with wearing the same sweatshirt and sweatpants to school everyday?" I never understood her comment until high school. Yeah, I was slow at learning how to dress myself. Thanks to Kellie I had my first fashion tip.

High School

Girls in high school were even more attractive than the ones in middle school. They wore nice matching outfits and some even knew how to put on make-up. I still had no clue what having a girlfriend meant or how to go about getting one. Then again I wasn't interested enough to take action. I mean what are you supposed to do with a girlfriend? Eat lunch together? Do math homework? Talk on the phone?

It was during this time that some girls started avoiding me. At first I couldn't figure out why, but later on, I figured it out. They thought I was interested in them and got turned off. Was I interested? Probably. But c'mon, even if I was, it wasn't like I was going to do anything about it. What was I gonna do? Have a girlfriend?

College

I had a few girl pen pals in college. Every week I'd trade letters with them. I appreciated this because girls rounded out the rough edges of guys in ways other guys just can't. Guys can be pretty insensitive and clueless, not on purpose, but, because that's who they are.

When I was a freshman, countless older people told me if I wanted to make friends I needed to initiate conversations. I decided to take that advice to heart so out of the blue I asked Carrie, a girl I just met, for her e-mail so we could do lunch. I must have freaked her out because not only did she never respond to my e-mail, she avoided me for the rest of the quarter… actually for the rest of my college years and beyond to be precise. Ooops. So much for taking people's advice.

There were probably other girls that I freaked out also. If you are reading this and are one of them, I'm sorry. I just didn't know better. I also want to thank you because I wouldn't be where I am today if I didn't learn from all those experiences. I'm not saying that you were training grounds for me. I'm just saying… ummm, I better stop here. I could get in trouble for continuing. OK. Next stage…

Real World

Right after college, I began to write down everything I learned about boy-girl relationships (BGRs). I hope that *Peanut Butter & Jelly* would speed up the learning curve for many single guys and girls.

I'm glad there are girls in this world. I think the world is a much better place because of them. The world is softer, more pleasant, nicer, cleaner, prettier, more decorative, festive, energetic, emotional, and many more things thanks to girls.

As much as I've learned, there are some things about a girl I may never understand. These include:

1) Why she likes flowers so much?
2) Why she's so concerned about her weight?
3) Why she's so concerned about her skin?
4) Why she's so concerned about her hair?
5) Why she's such a romantic nut?
6) Why she likes chick flicks so much?
7) Why every story has to end with "happily ever after"?
8) Why she never brings enough layers of clothes with her?
9) Why she's so into hearing and spreading stories about other people's lives?[80]
10) Why she's so worried about everything?
11) Why she loves puppies?
12) Why she loves desserts?
13) Why she happens to notice all the human beings under three feet tall wherever she goes?
14) Why she goes bananas about giving and receiving gifts?
15) Why she cares so much about cleanliness?
16) Why she likes shopping so much?
17) Why she is such a sucker for kind words?
18) Why she asks you to do favors she could easily do herself?
19) Why ambiance is so important to her?
20) Why when she asks you for your opinion she is actually hoping you would agree with her (If you don't believe me, the next time a girl asks you what you think about a movie she loves, tell her that you thought the lines were cheesy and the acting fake. Watch her reaction.)?
21) Why she calls you pessimistic when you are actually realistic?

---

80 Some people call this gossip.

22) Why she always has to have something swishy and soft with her all the time like a teddy bear?

There are many more things about girls I may never understand, but I guess that's OK. That makes them a mystery and it keeps us, guys, guessing and trying to figure them out, which I think girls like.

3) Recommended Resources

Communication

- *The Book of Questions* (NY: Workman Publishing Company, 1987), Gregory Stock
- *The Complete Book of Questions: 1001 Conversation Starters for Any Occasion* (Grand Rapids, MI: Zondervan, 2003), Garry Poole
- *The Fine Art of Small Talk: How to Start a Conversation, Keep it Going, Build Networking Skills—and Leave a Positive Impression!* (NY: Hyperion, 2005), Debra Fine
- *How You Can Be More Interesting* (Beverly Hills, CA: LPC Group, 2000), Edward De Bono
- *How to Talk to Anyone, Anytime, Anywhere: The Secrets of Good Communication* (NY, NY: Three Rivers Press, 1995), Larry King
- *How to Win Friends and Influence People* (NY: Pocket, 1998), Dale Carnegie
- *I Love You, Ronnie* (NY: Random House, 2000), Nancy Reagan
- *The Pocket Guide to Making Successful Small Talk : How to Talk to*

Anyone Anytime Anywhere About Anything (New Albany, IN: Pocket Guide Company, 1999), Bernardo J. Carducci

Dating/Relationships

- *The Art of the Chase* (Orange, CA: Revell, 2007), Hayley & Michael DiMarco
- *The Art of the First Date* (Orange, CA: Revell, 2006), Hayley & Michael DiMarco
- *The Art of Rejection* (Orange, CA: Revell, 2006), Hayley & Michael DiMarco
- *The Art of Small Talk* (Orange, CA: Revell, 2007), Hayley & Michael DiMarco
- *Dateable* (Grand Rapids, MI: Revell, 2003), Justin Lookadoo & Hayley Morgan
- *Define the Relationship* (Colorado Springs, CO: WaterBrook Press, 2004), Jeramy & Jerusha Clark
- *The Dirt on Dating* (Orange, CA: Revell, 2005), Hayley DiMarco
- *The Dirt on Breaking Up* (Orange, CA: Revell, 2004), Hayley DiMarco & Justin Lookadoo
- *For Men Only* (Atlanta, GA: Multnomah, 2006), Shaunti & Jeff Feldhahn
- *For Women Only* (Atlanta, GA: Multnomah, 2004), Shaunti Feldhahn
- *Godly Men Don't Exist*, Brenda Jung
- *Let Me Be A Woman* (Wheaton, IL: Tyndale, 1976), Elisabeth Elliot
- *The Mark of a Man* (Grand Rapids, MI: Revell, 1981), Elisabeth Elliot
- *Marriable* (Grand Rapids, MI: Revell, 2005), Hayley & Michael DiMarco
- *Men Are From Mars, Women Are From Venus* (NY, NY: HarperCollins, 1993), John Gray
- *the one?—is there such a thing and how would I know*, Mary Ann Nguyen Kwok

Dating Blogs:

- www.xanga.com/Tom_Martin
- www.xanga.com/whatwomenwant
- www.xanga.com/DefineTheRelationship
- www.xanga.com/mileschen

About the Illustrator

AUDREY JUNG lives in Los Angeles, California. She attends Fashion Institute of Design and Merchandising specializing in visual communications. Audrey hopes to become a set designer or a matte painter for the backgrounds of fantasy movies. She enjoys playing tennis, listening to her ipod, watching Pixar movies, painting, drawing, eating spinach ravioli, wood sculpting, and hopes to live in Oregon one day. She would love to hear from you.

JungAudrey@aol.com
jungaudrey.blogspot.com

About the Writer

MIKE TOY lives in San Francisco, California. He enjoys playing beach volleyball, hiking, camping (at nice hotels), eating shrimp, drinking strawberry milkshakes, watching his favorite movie *The Lord of the Rings* again and again, watching Hong Kong and Taiwanese music videos, karaoke, seeing the sun sink into the California horizon, directing children on making sandcastles, creative writing, joking around, traveling the world, chit-chatting, making new friends, taking people on an unofficial San Francisco tour, and daydreaming. Mike would love to hear from you.

pbjbook@gmail.com

Made in the USA
Lexington, KY
18 December 2010